Hiltm:

THE DIARY OF ANNE FRANK

AND OTHER PLAYS ABOUT COURAGE

W9-BDP-477

SCHOLASTIC INC.

Editor: Katherine Robinson
Editorial Director: Eleanor Angeles
Art Director and Designer: Marijka Kostiw

ISBN 0-590-34550-8

12 11 10 9 8 7 6 5 4   9/8 0 1/9

Printed in the U.S.A.   28

CONTENTS

THE KARATE KID

a screenplay by Robert Mark Kemen

CHARACTERS

DANIEL LaRUSSO, a high school student
LUCILLE, his mother
FREDDY, a 16-year-old who lives in their building
MIYAGI, the maintenance man for the building
JOHNNY, a student of the Cobra Kai Karate School
BOBBY, another student of the Cobra Kai
ALI, Johnny's former girlfriend
SUSAN, Ali's friend
KREESE, teacher of the Cobra Kai Karate School
REFEREE, official at a karate tournament
ANNOUNCER, another official at the tournament

It is a hot August day in the San Fernando Valley in California. Daniel and his mother arrive at an apartment building. Their car is loaded with luggage.

LUCILLE: Just look! Do you know what this means?

DANIEL: Yeah. Now I have to watch out for earthquakes and falling coconuts.

LUCILLE: Wise guy. It means no more freezing winters in New Jersey.

DANIEL: I like winters.

LUCILLE: Hey, this is the Garden of Eden. And we're in Apartment 2-D.

(Lucille carries a carton into the building. Daniel grabs a carton and follows. He kicks open the front door, pretending to be a karate expert. The door knocks down Freddy, who is Daniel's age.)

DANIEL: I'm sorry.

FREDDY *(getting up)*: It's okay. Are you the new people in Apartment 2-D?

DANIEL: Yeah.

FREDDY: I'm Freddy Fernandez. Was that karate you just did?

DANIEL: Yeah.

FREDDY: Have you ever used it?

DANIEL *(faking it)*: A couple of times.

FREDDY: Maybe you could teach me some time.

DANIEL: Sure. *(He goes on up to his apartment and enters.)*

LUCILLE: You know, this was really the right move. I've never felt so positive about anything in my life. By the way, the kitchen faucet is—

(Daniel has just turned on the faucet and is sprayed with water.)

DANIEL: Good timing, Ma.

LUCILLE: There's a maintenance man for the building. See if you can find him, okay?

(When Daniel enters the maintenance shed, he sees dozens of tiny trees growing in low pots. Then he sees an old man holding a pair of chopsticks and watching a fly buzzing around.)

DANIEL *(unsure)*: We're the new people in 2-D. *(The old man keeps watching the fly.)* Our faucet is leaking. Can you fix it?

(The old man stabs at the fly with the chopsticks, but misses.)

DANIEL: Can I tell my mom when?

MIYAGI: When what?

DANIEL: When you'll fix the faucet.

MIYAGI: After.

DANIEL: After what?

MIYAGI *(watching the fly)*: After.

(The next day, Daniel plays soccer with Freddy and some other boys at the beach. Daniel keeps looking at Ali, who is sitting with some girls nearby.)

FREDDY *(tossing the ball toward Ali)*: Make a move, Karate Kid.

(Ali picks up the ball and tosses it to Daniel. Daniel bounces it from knee to knee, then to his head.)

ALI: Is that hard to learn?

DANIEL: Not really.

ALI: Will you show me?

DANIEL: Sure. Hey, what's your name?
ALI: Ali—with an "i."

(*Just then, Johnny and the Cobras appear. Ali doesn't want to talk to Johnny, so she turns up her radio. Johnny throws it in the sand. Daniel starts to pick it up.*)

JOHNNY: Don't touch it.

(Daniel hands it to Ali anyway. Johnny grabs it and rams it into Daniel's chest. Daniel jumps at him, but Johnny steps aside and Daniel falls down.)

ALI: Stop it!

JOHNNY *(acting innocent)*: I didn't do anything.

(Daniel charges again. Johnny catches him with a kick.)

JOHNNY: Have you had enough, hero?

FREDDY *(to Daniel)*: Drop him, man! Karate him!

ALI: Stop!

(Johnny kicks Daniel in the face. Daniel falls down and doesn't move.)

FREDDY: Hey, man, you told me you knew that stuff.

ALI *(going to Daniel)*: Let me help you up.

DANIEL: Leave me alone.

(The kids leave, one by one.)

(After school the next day, Daniel practices karate kicks in his living room. He refers to an instruction book. There's a knock on the door. Daniel lets in Miyagi.)

MIYAGI: I came to fix the faucet. *(He sees the instruction book.)* Are you learning karate from a book?

DANIEL: Yeah.

MIYAGI: How did you get that black eye?

DANIEL: I fell off my bike.

MIYAGI: And you didn't hurt your hands?

(Daniel looks at his hands, then at the old man. He goes back to practicing kicks. Miyagi starts to fix the faucet.)

(Later, Daniel sees the Cobra Kai Karate School near the restaurant where his mother works. He goes inside the karate school and sees 15 students facing their teacher, John Kreese.)

KREESE *(sternly)* : We do not train to be merciful. Mercy is for the weak. If a man faces you, he is an enemy. An enemy deserves no mercy. Now, Mr. Lawrence, warm them up.

(A student with a black belt springs to the front. He bows. Then, as he turns, Daniel sees that's it's Johnny.)

9

(Next we see Daniel riding his bike along a lonely road. Johnny and three Cobras ride up on motorcycles. Johnny starts to edge Daniel off the road.)

DANIEL: I'm sorry. Okay?

(Johnny's motorcycle hits Daniel's bike. Daniel goes off the road and crashes down a rocky hill.)

(When Lucille gets home from work, she sees Daniel arriving home. His clothes are torn. His face and hands are cut. He is pushing his broken bike along.)

LUCILLE: Daniel, what happened?

DANIEL *(flinging down the bike)*: I've got to learn karate.

LUCILLE: Did some kids at school do this? *(He doesn't answer.)* Should I call the dean?

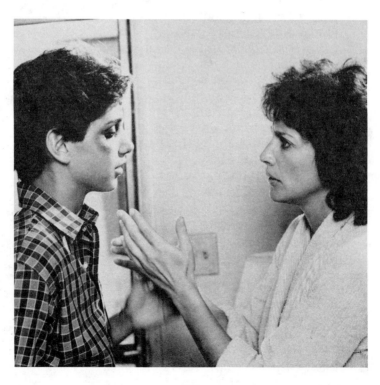

DANIEL: No!

LUCILLE: Fighting is not the answer. It will blow over.

DANIEL: Yeah. Sure.

(Miyagi watches from his shed. He has heard everything.)

(The next day, Daniel finds his bike at his front door. It's as good as new. He goes to Miyagi's shed.)

DANIEL: Did you fix my bike? *(Miyagi nods.)* Thank you!

MIYAGI: You're welcome.

DANIEL *(looking at the tiny trees growing in pots)*: How did these trees get so small?

MIYAGI: I trained them, clipping here and tying there.

DANIEL: Where did you learn that?

MIYAGI: In Okinawa, where I was born. It's an island between Japan and China. *(He sees Daniel admiring the trees.)* They're called *bonsai*. My father taught me.

DANIEL: Was he a gardener?

MIYAGI: No, a fisherman.

(Lucille enters the shed.)

LUCILLE: Daniel, I saw your bike outside. You fixed it!

DANIEL: Mr. Miyagi fixed it.

LUCILLE *(to Miyagi)*: Thank you. How much do I owe you?

MIYAGI: Nothing. It's my pleasure.

LUCILLE: Thank you very much.

(It's a Friday night about six weeks later. From his apartment, Daniel watches Freddy and some other kids leave the building wearing Halloween costumes and laughing. Daniel, looking gloomy, goes to Miyagi's shed.)

MIYAGI: I just passed the school. It looks like a party.

DANIEL: I'm not going.

MIYAGI: You are by yourself too much.

DANIEL: I'm not by myself. I'm with you. Besides, I don't have a costume.

MIYAGI: Would you go if you had a costume?

DANIEL: Do you remember my bike accident? Well, it wasn't an accident. Unless I went to the dance as the Invisible Man, I'd be asking for trouble.

(Miyagi sees some shower heads hanging from the rafters. He gets an idea.)

(Next we see the school gym, decorated for the dance. Students in costumes are dancing to rock music. A "shower"—with a curtain, shower head, and gray yarn for water—appears. Daniel peeks out of the curtain. He sees Ali, opens the curtain, then closes it around her.)

ALI *(pleased)*: I've never danced with a shower before. Where have you been hiding?

DANIEL: I've been busy.

ALI: I'm glad you got unbusy.

DANIEL: Me, too.

(A giant chicken has been watching the shower. It takes an egg from the basket it carries and tosses it over the top of the shower. It breaks over Daniel's head.)

(Daniel washes the egg off in the lavatory. He notices that Johnny is smoking in one of the stalls. Daniel drapes a hose over the top, turns on the water, and quickly leaves. The Cobras are standing in his path. He runs out to the parking lot, tearing off his costume. The Cobras follow. Daniel starts to climb over a fence. Johnny, soaking wet, pulls him back.)

JOHNNY: You couldn't leave well enough alone. Now you're going to pay for it.

(The Cobras push Daniel around. Each time he passes Johnny, he gets a vicious kick. He finally falls down and doesn't move.)

JOHNNY: Get him up.

BOBBY: He's had enough.

JOHNNY: An enemy deserves no mercy.

BOBBY: Come on. He's had it.

JOHNNY *(like a robot)*: If a man faces you, he is your enemy. An enemy deserves no mercy.

(Two of the Cobras prop up Daniel against the fence.

Johnny is about to kick him again. A figure appears from nowhere and blocks the kick. Daniel passes out. One by one, the Cobras attack the stranger. One by one, they are knocked to the ground.)

(When Daniel opens his eyes, he is in Miyagi's shed.)

DANIEL: Where's the other guy? *(Then he realizes.)* You?

MIYAGI: Why not? Do you think I'm too old?

DANIEL: Why didn't you tell me you knew karate?

MIYAGI: You never asked.

DANIEL: Would you ever teach anyone?

MIYAGI: It depends on the reason.

DANIEL: How's revenge?

MIYAGI: Fighting is the last answer to a problem.

DANIEL: You don't understand. I keep getting stomped.

13

MIYAGI: That's because those boys have learned the wrong attitude. Karate should be used for defense.

DANIEL: Great. So all I have to do is straighten it out with their teacher. If I tried that, they'd kill me.

MIYAGI: They're killing you anyway.

DANIEL: Will you go with me?

MIYAGI: I should not get involved.

DANIEL *(angry)*: Well, thanks for nothing. You give advice, but you won't follow it yourself.

MIYAGI *(troubled)*: Okay, I'll go.

(At the Cobra Kai Karate School the next day, Johnny sees Daniel and Miyagi in the visitors' section.)

KREESE: We do not train to be merciful. Mercy is for the weak. Mr. Lawrence, why are you limping?

(Johnny whispers something to him. Kreese walks over to Daniel and Miyagi.)

KREESE *(glaring at Miyagi)*: I understand you jumped my student.

MIYAGI: I think he's got his facts mixed up.

KREESE: Are you calling my boy a liar?

MIYAGI: I'm not calling anyone anything. I just want them to leave this boy alone.

KREESE: Can't he take care of himself?

MIYAGI: One to one, yes. But four to one is not fair.

KREESE: We can fix that. Hey, kid, do you feel like matching Mr. Lawrence?

MIYAGI: No more fighting.

KREESE: This is a karate school, not a knitting class.

MIYAGI: Your student would have an advantage here.

KREESE: Then name a place.

(Miyagi points at a poster announcing the All-Valley Karate Championship.)

KREESE *(laughs)*: Okay. Is there anything else I can do for you?

MIYAGI: I want my student left alone to train.

KREESE: Okay. But if you don't show, it's open season on you both.

(Miyagi bows. Then he and Daniel leave.)

DANIEL *(upset)*: I thought you were going to help me.

MIYAGI: I did. I saved you from three months of getting beaten up.

(They go to Miyagi's house. The yard is filled with old cars.)

DANIEL: I didn't know you were in the car business.

MIYAGI: Not everything is as it seems. *(He brings out a pail, sponges, rags, and car wax.)*

DANIEL: Do you think I can beat him?

MIYAGI: It doesn't matter if you win or lose. If you show a good fight, you'll get respect Then they

15

won't bother you. Now, I'll teach you karate. But you must do as I say without any questions. Is it a deal?

(Daniel puts out his hand to shake. Miyagi hands him a soapy sponge.)

MIYAGI: Wash the cars. Then wax them. Rub the wax on in small circles, from left to right. Each circle, breathe in and out. Wipe the wax off with small circles, from right to left. Again, breathe in and out. The breathing is important.

(Late that night, all the cars are shining. Daniel, who is exhausted, goes into Miyagi's house, expecting to be praised. The old man is asleep.)

(At school on Monday, Ali is upset when she sees Daniel's bruises.)

ALI: I'm going to find King Jerk. This has to stop.

DANIEL: It's okay. We've got an agreement. They promised not to beat up on me, and I promised not to get blood on their clothes.

ALI: You're unreal.

DANIEL: What am I supposed to do? Moan about it?

ALI: Anybody else would.

DANIEL: Who would listen?

ALI: I would.

DANIEL: Well, do you feel like listening Saturday night?

ALI: Sure. I have to have dinner with my parents at their country club. But I'll be finished by 9:30. You can meet me outside.

(She smiles and leaves. Then Daniel sees Johnny.)

JOHNNY: Don't push it, punk.

(That afternoon, Daniel finds that Miyagi has built a wooden deck behind his house. Miyagi gives him some sandpaper. He shows Daniel how to sand the wood in circles, first one way and then the other.)

DANIEL: Wouldn't it be easier to go back and forth?

MIYAGI: Yes, but you must work in circles.

18

(That night, Daniel finishes sanding the deck. Miyagi tests the smooth surface with his bare feet. Then he bows to Daniel.)

MIYAGI: Good. Come over tomorrow at 6:00 a.m.

(The next morning, Daniel finds him trying to catch a fly with chopsticks.)

DANIEL: Wouldn't a flyswatter be easier?

MIYAGI: A person who can catch flies with chopsticks can do anything.

DANIEL: May I try?

(He takes the chopsticks. His hand shoots out at a buzzing sound. The buzzing stops.)

DANIEL: Hey, look at that!

MIYAGI: Beginner's luck.

DANIEL: Does that mean I can accomplish anything?

MIYAGI: Yes. But first paint the house. *(He has seven cans of paint lined up.)* Paint up and down, with one hand and then the other. It's all in the wrist. And don't forget to breathe with each stroke.

(He leaves the house. When he returns that night, he carries a string of fish.)

MIYAGI: You missed a spot.

DANIEL *(angry)*: Why didn't you tell me you were going fishing? I would have gone, too.

MIYAGI: You're in karate training.

DANIEL: I'm being your slave is what I'm doing. I haven't learned a thing!

MIYAGI: You've learned plenty. Show me "wax on."

DANIEL: My arms ache too much.

(Miyagi rubs his hands together very fast. Then he puts them on Daniel's shoulders, pressing with his thumbs and palms. The ache disappears.)

DANIEL: How did you do that?

MIYAGI: Show me "wax on."

(Daniel makes perfect circles, from left to right. Miyagi throws a chest punch. Before Daniel realizes it, one of his hands blocks the punch. He smiles.)

19

MIYAGI: Now "sand the deck."
(Daniel makes perfect circles, lower down. Miyagi throws a stomach punch. Daniel blocks it.)

MIYAGI: Now "paint the house."
(Daniel "paints" up and down. On an upstroke, he blocks a head punch. On a downstroke, he blocks a stomach punch.)

MIYAGI *(picking up his fish)*: Come back tomorrow. *(He goes inside his house.)*
(The next day, Daniel and Miyagi go to the beach. Daniel tries to keep his balance as waves crash over him. Down the beach, Miyagi is standing on a piling on one foot. When a wave breaks, Miyagi leaps over it, fires a kick, and lands on one foot again.)

DANIEL *(on the way home)*: What was that you were doing?

MIYAGI: It's called the crane technique.

DANIEL: Would you teach it to me?

MIYAGI: Learn to stand first. Then you can learn to fly. *(Daniel looks disappointed.)* That's nature's rule, not mine.
(On Saturday night, Daniel goes to meet Ali at a country club, where she's having dinner with her parents. When she doesn't appear outside at 9:30, Daniel is worried. He walks around the club house and enters the kitchen. He looks into the dining room and sees Johnny dancing with Ali. When Johnny sees Daniel, he kisses Ali.)
(There is a crash. Everyone turns to see Daniel and a waiter on the floor in the middle of broken dishes. Johnny laughs. Daniel gets up and runs out. Ali clips Johnny with a punch, then runs after Daniel.)

ALI *(calling)*: I want to explain. Would you listen?

DANIEL: And be lied to?

ALI: You're rude.

DANIEL: You mean I'm not good enough for you and your rich friends. *(He leaves.)*

21

(Miyagi takes Daniel rowing on a lake. Daniel puts all his strength behind the oars.)

MIYAGI: Stop!

DANIEL: Shouldn't I be practicing?

MIYAGI: You *are* practicing. Stand up. *(He rocks the boat, and Daniel falls into the water).* You're practicing how to stay dry.

(Daniel climbs back into the boat and stands again. He practices blocking punches while Miyagi rocks the boat.)

DANIEL: When am I going to learn how to punch?

MIYAGI: First things first.

DANIEL: But how can I score a point if I don't punch?

MIYAGI: How can you score if you're knocked down? Balance is the key.

(Later, they sit by a campfire.)

DANIEL: How come you left Okinawa?

MIYAGI: The Japanese Army wanted me.

DANIEL: You mean you ran away?

MIYAGI: I don't like fighting.

DANIEL: But you know karate. You like to fight.

MIYAGI: Is that what you think?

DANIEL *(thinking)*: No, I don't.

MIYAGI: Good. I think you're ready to learn how to punch.

(It is almost Christmas. In school one day, Johnny hands Daniel a sheet of paper.)

DANIEL: What's this?

JOHNNY: It's a release form. Your parents have to sign it before the tournament. That's so they'll know where to claim the body.

DANIEL *(as Johnny turns away)*: Hey! Do you get a kick out of doing this?

JOHNNY *(acting innocent)*: Doing what?

DANIEL: Trying to scare me. We both know you can stomp me. So why bother to rub it in?

JOHNNY: Maybe I like to.

DANIEL: Did you ever think your teacher might be wrong?

JOHNNY: Watch it, twerp!

(Later, Daniel sees Ali and her friend Susan at a video-game arcade. He goes over to Ali.)

DANIEL: Can we talk?

ALI: I have nothing to say.

DANIEL: I want to apologize.

ALI: What do you expect from me—cartwheels?

DANIEL: No, just a little courtesy. But I guess you save that for people at your country club.

(Ali walks away.)

SUSAN: What makes you so sensitive?

DANIEL: Huh?

SUSAN: She's never been anything but nice to you.

DANIEL: Yeah. She was so nice that she used me to get Johnny jealous.

SUSAN: She doesn't like him.

DANIEL: I never would have guessed it the way their faces were stuck together at the country club.

SUSAN: I guess you didn't stick around for the exciting conclusion.

DANIEL: What happened?

SUSAN: She hit him.

DANIEL *(amazed)*: Why didn't she tell me?

SUSAN: She shouldn't have to.

(Daniel rushes after Ali and catches up with her.)

DANIEL: I'm a jerk.

ALI *(suddenly smiling)*: Yes, you are.

(They both laugh. Everything is all right now.)

DANIEL: I'm in a karate tournament tomorrow.

ALI: I know.

DANIEL: I'll probably get killed in the first match.

ALI: So, we'll leave early.

(Late that night, Daniel asks his mother to sign the release form for the karate tournament.)

LUCILLE *(upset)*: This says I won't hold anyone responsible if you are injured. Are you crazy?

DANIEL: Ma, I have to do this.

LUCILLE: Do what? Get killed?

DANIEL: No one gets hurt.

LUCILLE: Then why do I have to sign? *(She crumples up the paper.)* Good night, Daniel.

(Later, we see Daniel smoothing out the crumpled paper.)
(The next day, Daniel, Ali, and Miyagi arrive at the tournament. Karate students are lined up on the gym floor.)

ANNOUNCER *(over the public-address system)*: Attention please. Contenders, go to your assigned rings.

(The contenders go to different rings. Daniel finds himself in a ring facing Jimmy, one of the Cobras.)

REFEREE *(to Daniel and Jimmy)*: My word is law. If you don't listen, you're out. If you make contact, except in a clash, you're out. If you strike the knees, the throat, the eyes, you're out. Now, bow. Get set. Begin.

(Jimmy charges with a series of punches. None of them catches Daniel, but he is driven out of the ring.)

REFEREE: LaRusso, try to stay in the ring. Continue.

(Jimmy delivers a kick. Daniel blocks it and fires a punch.)

REFEREE: Point. LaRusso. Continue.

(Jimmy charges again. Daniel steps aside and kicks, stopping the charge.)

REFEREE: Point. LaRusso, the winner.

(Later, as Daniel starts his fifth match, Lucille runs into the gym. When she sees a boy about to kick Daniel's face, she is horrified. To her surprise, Daniel steps aside and scores with a light punch. She is impressed when he wins the match.)

ANNOUNCER: Ladies and gentlemen, the winner of the first semifinal match is John Lawrence of the Cobra Kai. The winner of the next semifinal will face Lawrence in the final match. Daniel LaRusso and Bobby Brown, please report to the center ring. *(As Bobby, a Cobra Kai, enters the ring, Kreese whispers to him.)*

KREESE *(whispering)*: Put him out of commission. *(He points to Bobby's knee.)*

BOBBY *(upset)*: But that would disqualify me.

(Kreese just stares at him. After the match begins, Bobby jumps high in the air. Instead of kicking out, his foot comes down on Daniel's knee. The crowd gasps. Daniel grabs his knee and falls. The crowd begins to boo.)

BOBBY *(to Daniel)*: I'm sorry. I'm sorry.

REFEREE *(pushing Bobby aside)*: Make way for the stretcher.

ANNOUNCER: Bobby Brown is disqualified. The winner is Daniel LaRusso.

(Bobby leaves the ring with tears in his eyes. He walks up to Kreese, unties his own belt, and drops it at Kreese's feet.)

(Daniel is carried to a dressing room. Miyagi rubs his hands together very fast. He presses Daniel's knee with his fingers. Daniel stands up and nods. They walk back to the gym—just as Johnny is about to accept the winner's trophy.)

ANNOUNCER: Hold on. Ladies and gentlemen, Daniel LaRusso is back on his feet! *(The crowd cheers.)* How's the leg, son? *(Daniel kicks twice.)* All right, it's time for the big event.

REFEREE *(to Daniel and Johnny)*: The first one to score three points wins. Bow. Get ready. Begin.

(Daniel scores two points right away. Kreese calls time.)

KREESE *(to Johnny)*: Sweep his bad leg. *(Johnny frowns.)* Do you have a problem?

JOHNNY: No, sir.

(Johnny "sweeps" a foot that catches Daniel just below his bad knee. As Daniel loses his balance, Johnny lands a punch and scores a point. Now Daniel is limping. Another sweep at Daniel's bad leg, followed by a kick, sends Daniel down. He is in a lot of pain.)

REFEREE: Two to two. Match point. Get ready. Continue.

(Daniel raises his bad leg and stands in the crane position. Miyagi smiles. Johnny looks confused.)

KREESE: Finish him.

(Johnny charges. Daniel leaps straight up, with his leg tucked in. Then he kicks, catching Johnny on the jaw. Then Daniel falls down.)

REFEREE: Point. LaRusso, the winner! *(He raises Daniel's arm.)*

27

JOHNNY *(to Daniel)*: Good match.

(Later, Daniel, Lucille, Ali, and Miyagi leave the gym.)

LUCILLE: We'll celebrate at our apartment. I'll go on ahead and get some lobsters ready. *(She kisses Daniel.)* You're marvelous. *(She turns to Miyagi.)* So are you. Don't be long. *(She leaves.)*

(Miyagi walks toward the parking lot. Daniel and Ali follow him. They see the Cobra Kai students getting into Kreese's van. Johnny is last in line.)

KREESE *(to Johnny)*: Beat it.

JOHNNY: I tried.

KREESE: I had him crippled, and you *still* couldn't beat him.

JOHNNY: It wasn't my fault.

KREESE *(grabbing Johnny)*: Are you suggesting it was mine?

MIYAGI: Why don't you pick on someone your own size?

(Kreese charges at Miyagi and throws a punch. Miyagi steps aside. Kreese turns and delivers a kick. Miyagi steps aside, and Kreese's foot crashes into his own van. Furious, Kreese throws another punch. Miyagi stops it with an open hand. Then his hand tightens around Kreese's fist, forcing Kreese to his knees. Kreese looks afraid.)

MIYAGI *(coldly)*: If a man faces you, he is an enemy. An enemy deserves no mercy.

(Daniel is shocked. The Cobras look worried. Miyagi's raised hand chops down toward Kreese's nose. Kreese closes his eyes. Miyagi's hand stops less than an inch from Kreese's face. But he flicks Kreese's nose with a finger. One by one, the Cobra Kai students leave, dropping their belts in front of Kreese. Daniel, Miyagi, and Ali walk away with Daniel's trophy.)

THE END

CHECKING THE FACTS

1. Why does Daniel want to learn karate?
2. According to Mr. Miyagi, why is revenge a poor motive for using karate? What is a good motive?
3. How does Mr. Miyagi train Daniel? Why does Daniel become impatient during the training?
4. Who wins the All-Valley Karate Championship? Why do the Cobra Kai students turn their backs on John Kreese, their teacher?

INTERPRETING THE PLAY

1. Mr. Miyagi says he left Okinawa just before being drafted into the Japanese Army, because he doesn't like fighting. Does this mean he is a coward?
2. Would you expect someone who is a karate expert to enjoy fighting? Contrast the attitudes of Mr. Miyagi and Mr. Kreese toward the use of karate.
3. In what ways does Daniel show courage?

WRITING

Imagine that you are Daniel. Write two entries in your journal. In the first one, tell why you are impatient with the way Mr. Miyagi is training you. In the second one, tell what you've learned from Mr. Miyagi.

WHERE THE LILIES BLOOM

a screenplay by Earl Hamner, Jr.

CHARACTERS

MARY CALL LUTHER, 14
DEVOLA LUTHER, 16
IMA DEAN LUTHER, 5
ROMEY LUTHER, 10
ROY LUTHER, their father
KISER PEASE
MRS. CONNELL
MR. CONNELL
GAITHER GRAYBEAL, 14
MISS FLEETIE, a teacher
GOLDIE PEASE
VOICE, singing

Fade in on the Great Smoky Mountains. The camera moves in on the Luther family. Mary Call and Romey are pulling a wagon up a mountain. The others follow. We hear a voice singing.

VOICE *(singing)*: I long to be where peace fills the air;
The wind sings softly in my ear;
I can hear the song that calls me there,
Where the lilies bloom.
I close my eyes, and I can see
A vision fair is leading me
To run through the green where I can be
Where the lilies bloom.

MARY CALL'S VOICE: Our family name is Luther. We have lived here for over 200 years. There has never been a more loving man than Roy Luther. He's our father. But since our mother died, he's been coughing his life away. More and more, I've had to take care of this family. My sister, Devola, is older. But she's never had a head for practical matters. Today we will gather lamb's-quarters. It is something like spinach.

ROY LUTHER *(picking an herb):* Wild marjoram. When it blooms, it smells as sweet as honey.

DEVOLA: It's got a pretty name.

ROY LUTHER: Means "joy of the mountain." If you were an herb, you'd be marjoram.

IMA DEAN: Am I one?

ROY LUTHER: No. You'd be meadowsweet. It looks like a rose, but it's got no thorns.

ROMEY: I bet you can't name me!

ROY LUTHER: You'd be a sassafras sapling. Mary Call? She'd be a yarrow.

MARY CALL: Yarrow's weak.

ROY LUTHER: It's stronger than it looks.

> *(Later, at the mountaintop, Romey, Devola, Ima Dean, and Mary Call are picking lamb's-quarters. Roy Luther is resting. He doesn't look well.)*

ROMEY: Mary Call, should I stay with Roy Luther?

MARY CALL: No. Just get back to work.

DEVOLA: He just asked a question, Mary Call.

MARY CALL: The air is thin up here. I want to get Roy Luther home before he has one of his spells.

> *(Later, they go back down the mountain. Roy Luther coughs now and then.)*

MARY CALL'S VOICE: If there's anyone we Luthers hate, it's Kiser Pease and his sister Goldie. Four years ago, they stole our land. They paid some taxes my father had let fall behind. Now we work as sharecroppers on the land we once owned. Goldie Pease has gone to live in Asheville. I wish Kiser had gone with her.

> *(They are now passing by Kiser's house.)*

DEVOLA: Do you want to rest now, Roy Luther?

ROY LUTHER: Not in front of Kiser Pease's house.

DEVOLA: He'd give us a drink of water.

MARY CALL: You heard what Roy Luther said. I'd die of thirst before I'd take water from that greasy outlaw!

DEVOLA: Kiser's not a greasy outlaw!

(That night, Mary Call is in her room, writing at her desk.)

MARY CALL'S VOICE: There is a part of me known only to Miss Fleetie. She is a teacher at our school. And she suggested that I write my thoughts in a journal. Writing at the end of a day has become a secret joy. But I've begun to feel a deep fright. Roy Luther's health is getting worse.

ROY LUTHER *(in the doorway, whispering):* Mary Call?

MARY CALL: Papa?

ROY LUTHER: Sh!

(Roy Luther and Mary Call walk outside. He opens the shed and shows her a coffin.)

ROY LUTHER: It's made of chestnut. *(He locks the door.)* I want you to promise me some things, Mary Call. You're the strongest. I'm depending on you.

MARY CALL: Yes, Papa.

ROY LUTHER: When it comes my time to die, let me go real quiet. No doctor. No undertaker. No preacher. They just take money. *(Pause.)* Kiser Pease has his eye on Devola. Don't let him marry her.

MARY CALL: I'll never let him marry her! Anyway, you're going to get better, Roy Luther!

(Several days later, Roy Luther can't get out of bed. Mary Call sits by him.)

MARY CALL'S VOICE: We took turns keeping watch over Papa. At first, he couldn't eat. Then I made him some tamarack tea, and he seemed better.

(Romey and Mary Call are fixing the roof of the house. A truck drives up.)

ROMEY: Oh, oh. Kiser Pease!

(Kiser walks toward the front door. Mary Call and Romey start down from the roof. Devola comes outside.)

DEVOLA: Hey, Kiser! I'm right glad to see you.

KISER: Uh, how you been keeping?

MARY CALL *(walking over)*: She's been keeping just fine. So we don't have to stand around yammering about it.

KISER: Mary Call, I sure do pity the man you marry.

MARY CALL: I feel the same for the person you hook up with, Kiser.

KISER: Mary Call, I had in mind talking to Roy Luther.

MARY CALL: Well, only a little while. He's been mighty sick.

(Kiser enters Roy Luther's bedroom. Mary Call stands in the doorway.)

KISER: How you doing, Roy Luther? *(There is no answer.)* There's been some hard feelings between you and me. But to my way of seeing it, I've done you a favor. Somebody else could have paid them taxes and kicked you off this place.

MARY CALL: What's your point, Kiser?

KISER: Roy Luther, I'd make Devola a good husband. *(Roy Luther tries to speak, but he can't.)*

MARY CALL: Roy Luther wants to say you can't marry Devola. He's against it. And I've promised never to let it happen. You better go. You're getting him upset. *(Kiser and Mary Call walk out to the front porch.)*

KISER: That's a mighty sick man in there.

MARY CALL: I've seen sicker get better.

KISER: I don't reckon he's got any money laid aside. *(Mary Call looks down.)* Well, the only thing I can think of is the county welfare.

MARY CALL: Luthers don't take charity.

KISER: Well, Roy Luther could have done a lot better with this place.

MARY CALL: Are you saying he could have worked harder?

KISER: No, just better.

MARY CALL: You get off our land!

KISER: Whose land? *(Pause.)* Well, I wish you luck. *(He leaves.)*

ROMEY *(to Mary Call)*: He isn't going to run us off, is he?

MARY CALL: No, Romey.

ROMEY: Have you ever seen a dead person?

MARY CALL: Mama.

ROMEY: What did she look like?

MARY CALL: Pale. Why?

ROMEY: Roy Luther is going to leave us, isn't he?

MARY CALL: He might.

ROMEY: If he does, what will we do?

MARY CALL: I don't know yet. But we're going to live!
(Next we see Mary Call and Romey with a box of potatoes. They knock on the door of Kiser's house. There is no answer.)

MARY CALL: Guess we'll just have to go find him.

ROMEY: I don't want to go in there.

MARY CALL: Do you want him to say we didn't bring him his share of the potatoes?
(They enter the house. Kiser is in a chair, very sick. He groans.)

MARY CALL: He's got pneumonia.

ROMEY: Are we going to do anything for him?

MARY CALL: Sure. We're going to keep him alive. He wouldn't be any good to us dead.

ROMEY: He's no good to us now.

MARY CALL: But he's going to be. Listen, we need lots of onions.

ROMEY: Oh, no. Not *that* cure!

MARY CALL: Run home and bring Devola here.
(Soon Romey, Mary Call, and Devola are lowering Kiser into a bathtub. Kiser tries to get out. But Romey sits on his legs. Mary Call opens Kiser's shirt. Devola starts putting cooked onions on his chest. Mary Call puts some on his head.)

ROMEY: Mary Call, this smell is terrible!

MARY CALL: You stay right there, Romey.
(The next morning, Kiser wakes up. Mary Call is sitting beside the bathtub.)

KISER: Mary Call? Is that you?

MARY CALL: Yeah, Kiser. You came close to dying. You're still real sick. If I went away now, you'd die!

KISER: Don't leave me!

MARY CALL: Well, I can't think of a reason to stay.

KISER: I'd pay you $10.

MARY CALL: I don't want your money. I want Roy Luther's land back . . . in our name, free and clear.

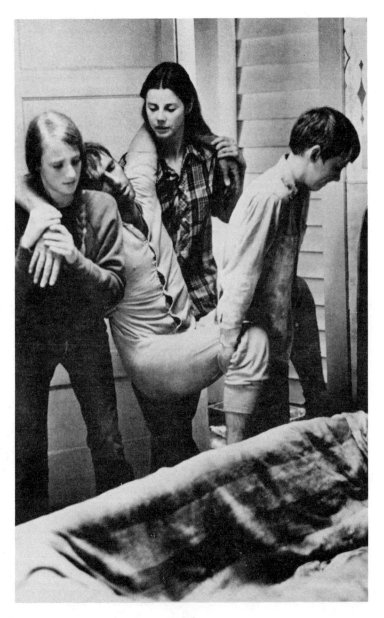

And I want you to sign a paper that says so. Let me read it to you. *(She reads.)* "I, Kiser Pease, say that the land I took from Roy Luther is his again. It belongs to the Luther family forever. Amen."

KISER: And if I sign, you won't let me die?

MARY CALL: I promise.

KISER *(signing):* Well, I trust you, Mary Call.

(Mary Call and Romey enter Connell's General Store. Mrs. Connell is behind the counter.)

MRS. CONNELL: Is that you, Mary Call? What brings you all in from the sticks?

MARY CALL: I need some supplies, Mrs. Connell.

MRS. CONNELL: I hear your daddy is on the go-down.

MARY CALL: He took a little spill.

MR. CONNELL *(entering):* Howdy, Mary Call. Hey, Romey. What can we do for you?

MARY CALL: I have a list, Mr. Connell.

MR. CONNELL *(taking the list):* All right.

MRS. CONNELL: Both my parents passed on when I was a little girl. I had to go live with a cranky aunt.

ROMEY: Nothing bad is going to happen to Roy Luther. He's going to be just fine.

MRS. CONNELL: That's for God to decide. And if He decides to take Roy Luther, you all are going to have to look for help. But don't you worry. There are institutions for folks like you.

ROMEY *(softly):* Old bat!

MR. CONNELL *(coming back with groceries):* Here you are, Mary Call. I've got to drive over to Banner Elk. Do you want a ride to the turn-off?

ROMEY: Yes, sir!

(They get into the truck. As Mr. Connell drives, he gives Mary Call a sheet of paper.)

MR. CONNELL: Show this to your daddy, Mary Call.

MARY CALL *(reading the paper):* A list of herbs. What is this for?

40

MR. CONNELL: A price list I got in Asheville. Your daddy will know what it is.

MARY CALL: You mean people pay for things you can pick up in the woods?

(Mr. Connell nods yes.)

ROMEY: What do they do with them?

MR. CONNELL: Same things your mama did. Make medicine. Your mama was the best wildcrafter in these mountains.

MARY CALL: We got a book at home. It's a guide to wildcrafting.

ROMEY *(looking at the paper)*: They pay 25 cents a pound for witch hazel!

MARY CALL: How come we didn't know about this before?

MR. CONNELL: Doctors have found out that there's worth in old remedies. If Roy Luther doesn't feel up to it, you children might go wildcrafting. You could make yourself a lot of money.

(Back at the Luther house, Mary Call goes to Roy Luther's bedroom.)

MARY CALL: Roy Luther! Mr. Connell gave us a price list of wildcrafting. Just wait . . . . *(She sees that Roy Luther is dead.)*

(Later, Romey, Mary Call, Devola, and Ima Dean bury their father. Then they stand by his grave.)

MARY CALL: I want each of us to say some good things.

ROMEY *(trying not to cry)*: He was good. He loved us all, fair and square. I was proud to have him for my daddy. And I hope he'll stay peaceful here.

MARY CALL *(tears running down her face)*: The Lord is your Shepherd now, Roy Luther. Be happy with Him. And don't worry about us.

IMA DEAN: Good-bye, Papa.

(Devola sings a song, "Been a Long Time Traveling.")

41

(Next we see the four young Luthers picking herbs and roots.)

MARY CALL'S VOICE: I have kept two of my promises to Roy Luther. No doctor. No undertaker. But what worries me is keeping Roy Luther's death a secret. If anybody finds out, they'll take us to the county home.

(Now we see the four children walking home. They carry sacks of herbs and roots. They see Kiser headed toward their house. Running, they get there before he does.)

MARY CALL: Get all this wildcrafting stuff out of sight! Kiser will want a share of it.

(They hide their sacks. Mary Call puts a pair of Roy Luther's long underwear into a pan of water. Then she carries it outside. Kiser has reached the porch.)

MARY CALL: Hi, Kiser

KISER: Hi, Mary Call. How are you doing?

MARY CALL: Just fine, Kiser.

KISER: Is your daddy in?

MARY CALL: He's real sick, Kiser. I'm his spokesman now. *(She hangs up her father's long underwear.)* I do all the planning.

KISER: You're enough to scare a man. Why can't you be sweet like your sister?

MARY CALL: Because sweet girls get themselves run over by people like you.

KISER: Mary Call, I aim to marry Devola.

MARY CALL: What have you got in those sacks?

KISER: I brought Devola a couple of hams. Mary Call, why don't you help me? You know how to talk to Roy Luther. I already gave him his land back. Tell him I'd take him for rides in my car.

MARY CALL: He's not used to cars.

KISER: Well, I'd bring it over and let him sit in it. I'd get him used to it. Then, after Devola and I are married, we'd take him for rides.

MARY CALL: You know I can't let you marry Devola. But as long as you're here, you might as well come in. And don't forget the hams. *(As she goes inside, Devola comes out on the porch.)*

KISER: How have you been keeping, Devola?

DEVOLA: All right, Kiser.

KISER *(giving her the sacks)*: Uh, I thought you might be hungry for some ham.

DEVOLA: Oh, that was real nice of you, Kiser!

(They sit down and begin to talk shyly with each other. Suddenly Ima Dean appears with some paper dolls. She shows them to Kiser.)

IMA DEAN: Look what I got!

KISER: Well, that's real nice. (*Ima Dean sits down and begins humming. Kiser takes a dime out of his pocket.*) Sis, if I give you this, will you go away?

IMA DEAN: But Mary Call told me to stay here!

MARY CALL (*walking out onto the porch*): I told Roy Luther you'd be bringing your car by. He said he'd be glad to sit in it.

KISER: If he's awake, I'd like a word with him.

MARY CALL: Well, he fell right back to sleep after I talked with him.

KISER: Well, I reckon I'll get along. You want to walk to the gate with me, Devola?

MARY CALL: Devola's got stuff to do in the house. But I'll be glad to walk you there, Kiser.

KISER: Never mind, Mary Call. I know the way.
(*Next we see the four children picking herbs and roots. Ima Dean and Romey stop working.*)

MARY CALL (*looking up*): Romey! Back to work! You, too, Ima Dean!

IMA DEAN: Mary Call, I'm tired.

MARY CALL: Don't give me any excuses.

ROMEY: Who put you in charge?

IMA DEAN: Yeah, Mary Call!

MARY CALL: I did.

DEVOLA: Leave them be, Mary Call.

MARY CALL: Have you got a better idea?

DEVOLA: You could be a little patient.

MARY CALL: I promised Roy Luther I'd keep this family together.

DEVOLA: We can't keep it hidden forever that Roy Luther is gone.
(*Next we see Roy Luther's grave. Mary Call puts some flowers on the grave.*)

MARY CALL'S VOICE: We have kept the death of Roy Luther a secret. With the money we earned wildcrafting, we have lived through the summer. I know Devola thinks I'm cruel. But it's the only way to stay out of the county home. School begins tomorrow. I'm uneasy. No one must learn that Roy Luther is gone.

(The next morning Devola and Mary Call are dressing Ima Dean for her first day of school.)

IMA DEAN: Can I take my rooster, Mary Call?

MARY CALL: I should say not. We'd better practice all the things I told you. Remember your answers?

IMA DEAN: Yeah!

MARY CALL: Ima Dean? How's Roy Luther?

IMA DEAN: He's just fine.

MARY CALL: Right. Romey, can I see you a minute? This doesn't look like Roy Luther's signature on your report card.

ROMEY: He's been sick, Miss Fleetie. His handwriting is kind of shaky.

MARY CALL: Good. Devola, this is Kiser. Is your daddy in?

DEVOLA: You can't see him, Kiser. He's asleep.

MARY CALL: What's he got? Sleeping sickness?

DEVOLA: He's on the mend, Kiser. Just go away before you wake him up.

(As Mary Call, Romey, and Ima Dean walk to school, Gaither Graybeal sees them.)

GAITHER: Where have you Luthers been all summer?

MARY CALL: We've been busy, Gaither. We're in the wildcrafting business.

GAITHER: The Connells say your dad has been bad off.

MARY CALL: Well, he was. But he's all better now.

GAITHER: Why don't you all come by after school?

MARY CALL: I'm afraid we'll have to get home. Maybe some other time.

(When they reach the school, the three Luthers enter and meet Miss Fleetie.)

MARY CALL: Hello, Miss Fleetie.

MISS FLEETIE: Well, there's three of you this year. How wonderful!

IMA DEAN: We're in the wildcrafting business.

MARY CALL: This is Ima Dean.

MISS FLEETIE: Welcome, Ima Dean. How's Roy Luther?

IMA DEAN: He's just fine.

(Later, after English class, Mary Call goes up to Miss Fleetie's desk.)

MARY CALL: Miss Fleetie, can Romey and I work in the cafeteria this year, so we can get free lunches?

MISS FLEETIE: I'll take care of it.

MARY CALL: I've got another problem, Miss Fleetie. I signed up for home ec. But somebody changed me to typing.

MISS FLEETIE: I'm that "somebody." Mary Call, you are good at writing.

MARY CALL: I've been keeping my journal.

MISS FLEETIE: I've had my heart broken in this room more times than I care to say. I've seen young men and women who could be doctors, lawyers, artists. I've seen them graduate, and not go on into the world. I'm not going to let that happen to you, Mary Call.

MARY CALL: I'm sorry, Miss Fleetie. I've got to go find Romey and Ima Dean. *(She walks outside.)*

GAITHER *(seeing Mary Call)*: May I carry your books, Mary Call?

MARY CALL: They're not heavy, Gaither.

GAITHER: Do you want to do homework together? I can come over after supper.

MARY CALL: I did mine in study period.

(Later, at the Luther house, Devola and Mary Call are drying roots before the fireplace. Romey is doing homework. A horn honks outside.)

ROMEY *(looking out the window)*: It's the Connells!

MARY CALL: Don't let them in till I'm ready.

48

(Romey goes outside. He meets Mr. and Mrs. Connell.)

ROMEY: Howdy, Mr. Connell! And how are you, Mrs. Connell?

MRS. CONNELL: I wheeze for days if I breathe too much of this mountain air.

ROMEY: Let me open the gate for you. *(He opens the gate slowly.)* You've got to open it a special way, or it will fall off.

MRS. CONNELL: Roy Luther ought to fix that gate. It could fall and hurt somebody.

ROMEY: He'll get around to doing it.

MRS. CONNELL *(looking around)*: This place has gone to pieces since your mother passed on. This yard was a flower garden in her day.

ROMEY: Uh, we've put in vegetables. Do you want to see the tomatoes?

MRS. CONNELL: I can't say as I do. You see one tomato plant, and you've seen them all.

ROMEY: Do you want to see Ima Dean's rooster?

MRS. CONNELL: I do not! I was pecked by a rooster when I was a little girl.

ROMEY: It sounds like an interesting story, Mrs. Connell. Tell me about it. *(He tries to block her from the porch.)*

MRS. CONNELL: Romey, will you kindly step aside?

MARY CALL *(walking out onto the porch)*: Oh, I didn't know we had company!

MR. CONNELL: Not company, Mary Call, just us Connells.

MRS. CONNELL *(giving a package to Mary Call)*: Bread. It's for Roy Luther.

MARY CALL: Well, he'll like that.

MRS. CONNELL: I want to take a look a him.

MARY CALL: Well, he's asleep right now. But you all have a seat on the porch.

MRS. CONNELL: I'd rather sit inside, if it's all the same to you.

MARY CALL: Come on in.

(They enter. Roy Luther's sweater has been placed on a chair.)

DEVOLA: Well, I didn't know we had company.

MR. CONNELL: We're not company, Devola. We just brought your daddy some bread.

MARY CALL: I told them Roy Luther was asleep. He *is* still sleeping, isn't he?

DEVOLA: Yeah. I just checked a minute ago.

MRS. CONNELL: Roy Luther must still be poorly. Of course, he never was what I'd call a tower of strength, not a practical man at all.

DEVOLA: Just because a body's got faults is no excuse not to love him.

MRS. CONNELL: Devola, I used to worry about you. You were dreamy like your daddy. But you're turning into a regular *person.*

(The next day Kiser drives his car into the Luther yard. Mary Call and Romey go out to meet him.)

KISER: I'm on my way to Wilkes County. Do you want to bring Roy Luther out here so he can sit in my car?

MARY CALL: He's asleep.

KISER: Well, I'll just leave her here then. *(He locks the doors.)* But she's going to stay locked.

MARY CALL: Devola will be awfully put out. She planned on listening to the radio.

KISER: Where is Devola?

ROMEY: Taking a bath. Do you want me to call her?

KISER: Oh, no! *(He tosses the keys to Mary Call.)* Tell her I don't want anybody in that car but her and Roy Luther. *(He leaves.)*

DEVOLA *(coming outside with Ima Dean):* Where's Kiser?

MARY CALL: Going to Wilkes County. But he said you could sit in the car and listen to the radio.

IMA DEAN: I want to hear the radio.

MARY CALL: Everybody get in.

(They all climb into the car.)

ROMEY: Where are we going?

MARY CALL: I don't know. *(She turns different knobs on the dashboard.)* Nothing's happening.

ROMEY: Turn the key!

MARY CALL *(laughs):* Oh, yeah.

(The car takes off, barely missing some trees. Mary Call gets the car on the road. They just miss hitting a bus, then a tractor. Off the road, they almost hit some cows. Finally, the car stops in a shallow creek.)

ROMEY: How are we going to get out of here?

MARY CALL: I'm not very good at going backward.

ROMEY: You're not very good at going forward, either!

DEVOLA: Do you want me to drive, Mary Call?

MARY CALL: Why didn't you tell me you could drive?
(Devola begins driving them home.)

MARY CALL: Devola, did Kiser show you how to drive?

DEVOLA: That's right.

(Next we see Mary Call, Devola, and Romey gathering herbs. Ima Dean is in Kiser's car, honking the horn.)

MARY CALL: Romey, go tell her to get back to work.

ROMEY: Can I take a break, too?

MARY CALL: A quick one.

ROMEY *(going to the car):* Knock that off, Ima Dean!

IMA DEAN: You're not the boss, Romey!

(Romey gets in the car and turns on the radio. Ima Dean honks the horn in rhythm to the music.)

MARY CALL *(angry):* A person can take only so much!
(She goes to the car and yells at Ima Dean.) One more honk out of you, and I'm going to spank you!

ROMEY: She's only a child, Mary Call.

MARY CALL: And I'm only 14! Now, go get me a fresh sack.

ROMEY: Go get it yourself. I'm not your slave!

DEVOLA: Mary Call? I'm going to take them for a ride and get them calmed down.

51

MARY CALL: You do that, Devola. I don't care if you never come back!

(Devola drives off with Ima Dean and Romey. Mary Call is so angry that she runs into a swarm of bees. When she gets home, she is covered with bee stings. Kiser is sitting on the porch.)

KISER *(laughing)*: Mary Call! What have you got yourself into now?

MARY CALL: Very funny!

KISER: I wanted to speak to Roy Luther, but the door was locked. So I went around and looked in his window. He isn't in there.

MARY CALL: Well, he must be off on one of his car rides. *(They hear a car.)* That must be Luther now.

(Devola drives up with Ima Dean and Romey.)

DEVOLA: Mary Call, what happened to you?

MARY CALL: I got too friendly with a bunch of bees. Where is Roy Luther?

ROMEY: We couldn't get him to come home with us. He got tired of hearing Ima Dean whine.

KISER *(taking a small pig from his truck)*: Hey, Devola, I brought you something.

DEVOLA: Thank you, Kiser!

MARY CALL: Kiser? You can take your car home now.

KISER: No. Devola can keep on driving it. But she ought to have a license.

MARY CALL: Well, you can take her to get one.

KISER: Good. Devola likes that pig, doesn't she?

MARY CALL: Yeah. She likes most any animal.

KISER: Huh?

MARY CALL *(laughing)*: She likes cows, too.

(Early the next morning, Kiser arrives with a cow.)

KISER: Devola, she's for you.

DEVOLA: She's so sweet. Thank you, Kiser.

KISER: Mary Call, I want to talk to Roy Luther.

MARY CALL: Roy Luther's not here this morning. He's digging roots.

KISER: This early in the morning? *(Mary Call smiles sweetly. Kiser turns to Devola.)* Get in the truck.

DEVOLA: Why can't we take the car?

KISER: I taught you to drive on the truck, honey. It will make the test easier for you.

MARY CALL: Bring her home before dark, Kiser. Roy Luther may be queer in the head. But he still knows how to use a shotgun!

(Later, Romey, Ima Dean, and Mary Call are walking home from school.)

ROMEY: What did I do?

MARY CALL: You fell asleep in history!

ROMEY: So Miss Fleetie told you, huh?

MARY CALL: It's lucky she didn't try to tell Roy Luther. Do you want us to end up in the county home?

ROMEY: No boss there could be worse than you are!

MARY CALL: You stay awake from now on!

ROMEY: What do you think I am—a machine that doesn't need sleep? Wake up, Romey! Build a fire, Romey! Bring in some wood, Romey! Do your homework, Romey!

MARY CALL: And you're going to have to bring up your grades.

ROMEY: When am I going to do that?

MARY CALL: In your spare time.

ROMEY: You make me laugh, Mary Call.

MARY CALL: I'm keeping promises. And I need you to help me, Romey.

ROMEY: Okay.

(It is now dark outside. Kiser has not yet brought Devola home. Mary Call and Romey are sitting on the Luther porch. A truck approaches.)

ROMEY: Here they come.

MARY CALL: Well, let me handle it.

(Devola gets out of the truck and runs forward.)

MARY CALL: All right, Devola! Where have you been?

DEVOLA *(tears running down her face)*: A truck ran over Kiser. They said it broke his leg. They took him to the hospital.

MARY CALL: I've wished Kiser some bad things. But not *that* bad.

DEVOLA: I didn't know what to do. So I came on home.

MARY CALL: Well, at least Kiser won't be bothering us for a while.

DEVOLA: I love him, Mary Call!

MARY CALL: I'm glad Papa can't hear you say that!

DEVOLA: Maybe Papa was wrong about Kiser.

(On a stormy night, Devola is drying off the pig in the Luther kitchen.)

MARY CALL: I will not live in the same house with a pig!

DEVOLA: Mary Call, he's just a baby.

(Romey enters with the cow.)

MARY CALL: Romey! No!

ROMEY: Mary Call, she won't take up much room.

MARY CALL: Romey, cows love water.

ROMEY: What if this cow got hit by lightning?

MARY CALL: Oh, Romey!

ROMEY: What?

MARY CALL *(tired)*: Nothing.

(Next we see Mary Call working in the school cafeteria.)

MARY CALL'S VOICE: I kept prodding my family to do this and that. They hated me, and I hated myself. Something had flown out of my brother and sisters. I would try to get them to sing or laugh. But their spirits were down.

(The Luther children are in the Luther kitchen again.)

DEVOLA: I'd give anything for a Thanksgiving turkey.

MARY CALL: Take this squash. We'll boil it with some turnips and potatoes. It will be just great1

DEVOLA: When Roy Luther was alive, we always had more.

MARY CALL: Well, I can't argue with you about that.
(They hear a car outside.)

ROMEY *(looking out the window)*: It's Kiser's sister, Goldie Pease!
(Mary Call opens the door. Goldie enters.)

GOLDIE: Where's Roy Luther?

MARY CALL: He's sick.

GOLDIE: I want to talk to him.

MARY CALL: He's asleep.
(The pig comes downstairs.)

GOLDIE: Pigs in Kiser's house!

MARY CALL: It's just one pig, and it's not Kiser's house. He signed it back over to Roy Luther. I've got the paper.

GOLDIE: I'd like to see it.

MARY CALL *(handing the paper to Goldie)*: Here.

GOLDIE *(trying to open Roy Luther's bedroom door)*: Roy Luther! *(The door is locked.)* This paper is worthless! You hear me?

MARY CALL: Sometimes he doesn't answer.

GOLDIE: He's always been queer in the head.

MARY CALL: Don't you talk about my papa like that!

GOLDIE: Roy Luther! I know you can hear me! I want you Luthers out of this house in 48 hours!

MARY CALL: But the paper is legal. Kiser signed it.

GOLDIE: It's worthless! Just like Kiser!
(Mary Call visits Kiser in the hospital.)

KISER: Mary Call! I've been dying to see somebody. How have you been keeping?

MARY CALL: Fine, Kiser. My, you've turned thin.

KISER: Yeah. This place is killing my nerves. I'm sick, and nobody cares.

MARY CALL: Kiser, I've been thinking. How would you like to get married?

KISER *(surprised)*: I would! I'll be good to her. I'll be good to you all.

MARY CALL: Kiser!

KISER: I'll get you all another pig. And—

MARY CALL: Kiser! I'm not talking about you marrying Devola. I thought you might like to marry me.

KISER: You?

MARY CALL: I love you. And I want to marry you.

KISER: Mary Call! You don't love me.

MARY CALL: How do you know I don't?

KISER: Mary Call, you've got no more use for me than a clod of dirt.

MARY CALL: I have so got use for you! Kiser, you're making me mad now. I didn't come all this way to be insulted!

KISER: I haven't insulted you.

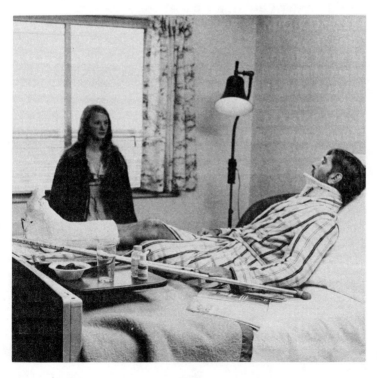

MARY CALL: You as much as called me a liar! Do you want to marry me or not?

KISER: No, I don't.

MARY CALL *(angry)*: You treasoner, you! You sent Goldie to tell us to get out! You—

KISER: I never even—

MARY CALL: And you sent Roy Luther into his grave! *(She starts to cry.)*

KISER: Mary Call? There's no use to bawl.

MARY CALL: Who's bawling?

KISER: Listen, honey. If I'd known that Roy Luther was dead—

MARY CALL: If you tell anybody, I'll blow your head off! *(She runs out.)*

KISER: Mary Call! Come back here, honey!
(Later, Mary Call is walking along a road. Kiser pulls up in his car. Mary Call keeps walking. Kiser drives slowly by her side.)

KISER: Mary Call. We've been looking high and low for you.

MARY CALL: Leave me alone, Kiser!

KISER: Listen. Your brother and sisters are worried to death about you.

MARY CALL: Oh, really? Well, it's time they did some worrying. I'm not going to do it for them anymore.

KISER: Mary Call, I'm taking you home.

MARY CALL: I'm going as far from this place as I can get. You try hustling up enough to eat for three kids. Try wildcrafting till dark to keep clothes on their backs. Try keeping it a secret you've buried your papa.

KISER: Mary Call—

MARY CALL: Try fighting off busybodies snooping around. Try to do homework while you're dead tired. *(She stops, and Kiser gets out of his car.)*

KISER: Mary Call. Roy Luther put a lot on you that didn't belong.

MARY CALL *(crying):* I let him down.

KISER: No, you didn't. You did all those things. And you did them better than a lot of grown people could have. *(He puts his arm around her shoulders.)* *(Next we see Devola and Kiser being married.)* *(Then we see Mary Call standing by Roy Luther's grave.)*

MARY CALL'S VOICE: Roy Luther was wrong about Kiser. He's a good man and will be gentle with Devola. I know now that you can love people even though they fail you. I still love Roy Luther. I always will. Perhaps that's the true test of love. Sometimes I feel something telling me to go to some far-off place. Once I've raised Romey and Ima Dean, I think I'll go. *(Fade out.)*

THE END

CHECKING THE FACTS

1. Why does Mary Call Luther hate Kiser Pease at first?
2. Why is Mary Call determined to keep Roy Luther's death a secret?
3. What is "wildcrafting"? How does this provide a source of income for the Luther family?
4. How does Mary Call get her family's land back from Kiser? Who threatens to take it away again?

INTERPRETING THE PLAY

1. Why does Roy ask Mary Call, not her older sister, to care for the family after his death? Do you think this was a wise decision?
2. How and why does Kiser's opinion of Mary Call change? How and why does Mary Call's opinion of Kiser change?
3. What responsibilities does Mary Call take on after her father dies? Of all the challenges and hardships she must face, which, in your opinion, takes the most courage?

WRITING

Suppose Roy Luther's death is discovered and his children are taken to the county home. Put yourself in Mary Call's shoes. Write a letter to the judge who will decide your fate. Try to convince the judge that you four children must stay together and that you can survive on your own.

THUNDER ON

SYCAMORE STREET

a teleplay by Reginald Rose

CHARACTERS

NARRATOR
ARTHUR HAYES
FRANK MORRISON
CLARICE MORRISON
ROGER MORRISON
PHYLLIS HAYES
JOSEPH BLAKE
ANNA BLAKE
JUDY BLAKE
MRS. CARSON
CHARLIE DENTON
FIRST MAN
SECOND MAN

PART ONE

NARRATOR: It is 6:40 p.m. on Sycamore Street in the village of Eastmount. There are three small houses—all alike—that belong to the Hayeses, the Morrisons and the Blakes. Arthur Hayes, a quiet man with glasses, is now on his way home. He pauses in front of his house. Something seems to be worrying him. Frank Morrison, a big loud-voiced man, comes down the sidewalk.

FRANK: Hey, Artie. How are you? *(Arthur seems not to hear him.)* Hey, wake up, boy.

ARTHUR: Oh, hello, Frank. Sorry. I didn't see you.

FRANK: Hey, wait till I tell Clarice. That diet she's got me on must be working. You have to look twice to see me! *(He laughs loudly.)* Say, isn't this late for you to be getting home?

ARTHUR: No.

FRANK: I wouldn't want you to be late tonight. You know what tonight is, don't you?

ARTHUR *(slowly)*: Yes, I know.

62

FRANK: Good.

NARRATOR: At this moment, Joseph Blake walks by. He lives in the third house. Neither Frank nor Arthur speaks to him. Arthur turns away, but Frank stares with hatred at Joseph.

FRANK: See you later, Artie.

NARRATOR: Each man goes into his house. Frank has a wife, Clarice, and a 10-year-old boy, Roger. When we next see him, they are at dinner.

FRANK: Do anything special today, Roger?

ROGER: Nope. Just hung around.

FRANK: Well, I don't know why you don't get out and do something. A boy your age . . . .

ROGER: Some kids dumped garbage on the Blakes' lawn again.

FRANK: What about you?

ROGER: Ah, what fun is that after you do it a couple of times?

FRANK *(chewing)*: Mm. Clarry, we'd better hurry.

CLARICE: There's plenty of time. I'm leaving the dishes till later.

FRANK: This really ought to be something tonight.

ROGER: What ought to be something? Where are you going?.

FRANK: We're going for a little walk.

ROGER: Well, why is everybody acting so funny?

FRANK *(sharply)*: I don't want to hear any more questions out of you. Your mother and I have some business to attend to. You mind yours. *(He gets up and lights a cigar.)*

CLARICE: Aren't you going to have some pie, Frank?

FRANK: I'll have it later.

ROGER *(low)*: I'm sorry, Dad.

CLARICE: How late do you think we'll be, Frank?

FRANK: I don't know.

CLARICE: Do you think I ought to pack a thermos of hot coffee? It's going to be cold.

FRANK: That's not a bad idea. *(Frank begins to show signs of being excited about the evening. He speaks almost to himself.)* I can't wait till I see his face. The nerve of him. *(Grins.)* What do you think he'll do when we all arrive at his house?

CLARICE *(looking at Roger)*: Frank . . . .

FRANK *(as Roger stares)*: Oh. Okay, Roger, you can turn on your program.

ROGER: Thanks, Dad. *(He goes to the TV and turns it on.)*

FRANK *(to Clarice)*: What are they saying on the block?

CLARICE: I didn't speak to anyone. I was ironing all day.

FRANK: Charlie Denton called me at the office. He says it's going to be 100 percent, every family on the block.

CLARICE: Well, that's good. Everyone should be in on this.

FRANK: Clarry, this is going to be a job well done. It's how you have to do these things. Everybody getting together fast—

CLARICE *(interrupting)*: I saw her today, hanging clothes in her yard as if nothing was wrong. She didn't even look this way.

FRANK *(walking around)*: This is something big, Clarry. We're getting action without a lot of sweet talk for once. That's the big part. There's too much sweet talk going on all the time. You're not supposed to hurt anyone's feelings. Well, that's tough, I say.

CLARICE *(looking at Roger)*: Frank . . . .

FRANK: He can hear! He's old enough. If you want something, you have to go out and get it! That's how this world is. Boy, I like this, Clarry. You know what it makes me feel like? It makes me feel like a man!

(The doorbell rings. Roger opens the door.)

ARTHUR: Roger, is your dad in?

ROGER: Sure. Come on in, Mr. Hayes. *(He goes back to watching TV.)*

FRANK: Hey, Artie. Come on in.

ARTHUR: Hello, Frank.

FRANK: What's up?

ARTHUR: I just wanted . . . to talk.

FRANK: Say, you look a little sick. What's the matter?

ARTHUR: Nothing. I've had an upset stomach for a couple of days. Maybe that's it.

FRANK: Probably a virus. Well, what's on your mind?

ARTHUR: What do you think about this thing tonight?

FRANK *(surprised)*: What do you mean what do I think about it?

ARTHUR: Well, I've been going over it all day, Frank. I talked with Phyllis before.

FRANK *(a little hard)*: And?

ARTHUR: And . . . well, look Frank, it's a pretty hard thing. Supposing it were you?

FRANK: It's not.

ARTHUR: I know. But if it were, how would you feel?

FRANK *(going over to Arthur)*: How would I feel, huh? It doesn't make any difference how I'd feel. Now let me ask you a question. Is he a lifelong buddy of yours?

ARTHUR: You know he's not, Frank.

FRANK: Do you know him to say hello to?

ARTHUR: That's not the idea.

FRANK: Artie, you don't even know the guy. Why are you getting yourself all upset? We all agreed, didn't we?

ARTHUR: Yes. Everybody agreed.

FRANK: Every family on Sycamore Street agreed.

ARTHUR: Well . . . I think we all ought to talk it over, maybe, and let it wait a few days.

FRANK: Artie, we talked it over. In a few minutes, we're starting. We expect to have a solid front— you included. You're my next-door neighbor, boy.

66

I don't want to hear people saying Artie Hayes wasn't there.

ARTHUR: Well, I don't know, Frank. I thought. . . .

FRANK: Go home, Artie. Don't worry about it. I'll see you in a few minutes.

NARRATOR: When Artie returns to his own home, his wife Phyllis is waiting for him.

PHYLLIS: Artie, are you all right?

ARTHUR: Yes, I'm fine.

PHYLLIS: We only have a couple of minutes, dear.

ARTHUR: I'm not going out there.

PHYLLIS: I'll get our coats.

ARTHUR: I said I'm not going!

PHYLLIS: I want to tell you something. I'm going to get our coats, and we're going to stand in the doorway of our house until it's 7:15.

ARTHUR: Stop it.

PHYLLIS: Then we're going to go into the street, and we're going to be just like everybody else on Sycamore Street!

ARTHUR (*shouting*): Phyllis! I've told you. I'm not going to be a part of this thing!

PHYLLIS (*after a pause*): Listen to me, Artie. We're going out there. Do you want to know why? Because we're not going to be next.

ARTHUR: You're out of your mind!

PHYLLIS (*shouting*): Sure I am! I'm crazy with fear, because I don't want to be different. I don't want my neighbors looking at us and wondering why we're not like them.

ARTHUR (*amazed*): Phyllis, you're making this up! They won't think that.

PHYLLIS: They will! We'll be the only ones who wanted to let an ex-convict live with us. They'll look the other way when we walk the streets. They'll become cold and nasty. (*She points at the Blake house.*) We'll be like them. We can't be different! We can't

67

afford it! We live on the good will of these people. Your business is in this town. Your neighbors buy us the bread we eat! Do you want them to stop?

ARTHUR: I don't know, Phyllis. I don't know what to think. I can't throw a stone at this man.

PHYLLIS: You can! You've got to, or we're done for here. *(He stares at her.)* Now, just wait. *(She runs to the closet and takes out their coats. She holds his for him.)* Put it on!

ARTHUR: I can't. They're people. It's their home.

PHYLLIS *(shouting)*: We're people, too! We've got to live here. Artie, we don't even know them. What's the difference what happens to them? What about us? *(He lets her put his coat on. He no longer knows the woman who is talking to him.)* There. It won't be long. I promise you. We'll be back in an hour, and it'll be over.

NARRATOR: She takes his arm and they wait in the doorway. From down the street, we hear the sound of tramping feet. The tramping grows louder. Phyllis and Arthur wait in silence. Now the crowd comes marching by, the Morrisons at the head. Charlie Denton, Frank Morrison's chief lieutenant, walks behind him. No one looks at the Hayeses. Slowly, Phyllis pushes Arthur forward. He steps out to join the others as if in a dream. Phyllis takes his arm as they join the marching mob.

PART TWO

NARRATOR: And now we go back to the beginning. Once again, it is 6:40 p.m. on Sycamore Street. Once again, Arthur Hayes pauses in front of his house, and Frank Morrison hails him.

FRANK: Hey, Artie. How are you? Hey, wake up, boy.

ARTHUR: Oh, hello, Frank. Sorry. I didn't see you.

FRANK: Hey, wait till I tell Clarice. That diet she's got me on must be working. You have to look twice to see me! *(He laughs loudly.)* Say, isn't this late for you to be getting home?

ARTHUR: No.

FRANK: I wouldn't want you to be late tonight. You know what tonight is, don't you?

ARTHUR *(slowly)*: Yes, I know.

FRANK: Good.

NARRATOR: At this moment Joseph Blake walks by. Neither Frank nor Arthur speaks to him. Arthur turns away, but Frank stares at Blake with hatred.

FRANK: See you later, Artie.

NARRATOR: Joseph Blake goes into his house. He is greeted by his six-year-old daughter Judy.

JUDY: Daddy! Daddy! *(He picks her up in his arms.)* We've got company.

JOE: Oh? Who is it, darling?

JUDY: A lady.

(Joe puts Judy down and goes into the living room. Anna and another woman, Mrs. Carson, are seated.)

ANNA *(nervously)*: Joe, this is Mrs. Carson.

JOE *(politely)*: Hello, Mrs. Carson. *(He kisses Anna on the forehead.)*

ANNA *(shakily)*: Joe, Mrs. Carson . . . *(She turns to Judy.)* Judy, go into your room. *(Judy goes.)* Joe, I don't understand it! Mrs. Carson says. . . . *(She is almost sobbing.)*

JOE *(putting an arm around her)*: Mrs. Carson says what?

ANNA: Joe, they're going to throw us out of our house. Tonight! Right now! What are we going to do?

JOE *(softly)*: Who's going to throw us out, Mrs. Carson?

MRS. CARSON: Well, as I told Mrs. Blake, I suppose it's none of my business. But I'm not the kind that thinks a thing like this ought to happen to people without them getting at least a . . . well, a warning. Do you know what I mean?

JOE: No, I don't know what you mean, Mrs. Carson. Did someone send you here?

MRS. CARSON: I should say not! If my husband knew I was here, he'd drag me out by the hair. No, I sneaked over here. I felt it was my duty. A man ought to have the right to run away, I say.

JOE: What do you mean run away, Mrs. Carson?

MRS. CARSON: Well, you know what I mean.

JOE: Who's going to throw us out?

MRS. CARSON: The people on Sycamore Street. They don't feel you ought to live here, because . . . well, I don't suppose I have to go into that.

JOE: I see. What time are they coming?

MRS. CARSON: About 7:15. *(She gets up.)* They're very angry people, Mr. Blake. I don't think it would be right for anyone to get hurt. If you take my advice, you'll just put some stuff together and get out. I don't think there's any point in calling the police. There are only two of them in town. I don't think they'd do much good against a crowd like this.

JOE: Thank you, Mrs. Carson.

MRS. CARSON: Oh, don't thank me. I don't know you people, but there's no need for anyone getting hurt as long as you move out. I don't know why a thing like this has to start up anyway. It's none of my business, but a man like you ought to know better than to come pushing in here . . . a fine neighborhood like this. After all, right is right.

JOE *(quietly)*: Get out, Mrs. Carson.

MRS. CARSON: What? Well, I never! You don't seem to know what I've done for you, Mr. Blake.

JOE: Get out of the house. *(He picks up Mrs. Carson's coat and gives it to her.)*

MRS. CARSON: Well, I should think you'd at least thank me. I might have expected this, though, from people like you!

ANNA: Mrs. Carson, please—

JOE: Anna, stop! *(He goes to the door and opens it.)*

MRS. CARSON *(as she goes out)*: I think you'll be getting what you deserve, Mr. Blake.

(Joe closes the door.)

ANNA: Joe, I'm scared. I'm so scared, I'm sick to my stomach. What are we going to do? We've only got 15 minutes!

JOE *(quietly)*: What do you want me to do? I can't stop them from coming here.

ANNA: Let's get out. We've got time. We can throw some things into the car.

JOE: Isn't it amazing? On a quiet street like this there are people with thunder in their hearts.

ANNA: Listen to me, Joe. We can stop at a motel.

JOE: We're staying.

ANNA *(afraid)*: No!

JOE: Anna, this is our home and we're staying in it. No one can make us get out of our home.

ANNA *(sobbing)*: Joe, do you know what a mob is like?

JOE: It's something I never thought of before. I guess a mob can do ugly things.

ANNA: Joe, you're talking and talking, and the clock is ticking so fast. Please, Joe. We can run. We can go somewhere else to live. It's not so hard.

JOE: It's very hard, Anna, when it's not your own choice.

ANNA: What else can we do? Stand here and fight them? We're not an army. We're one man, one woman, and a baby.

JOE: And this house belongs to us, not to anyone else.

ANNA: They don't care about things like that, Joe. Judy's six years old now. She's only really known you for a few weeks. We waited four years for you. She didn't remember you when you kissed her hello, but, Joe, she was so happy. What are you going to tell her when they set fire to her new house?

JOE: That her father fought like a tiger to stop them.

ANNA (crying): What good will that do? Joe, please—

JOE: Stop it! (Pause.) It's this way, Anna. We've just bought this house with money left from before . . . money you could have used many times. We have a mortgage and a very old car. We have my job.

ANNA (bitterly): Selling pots and pans at kitchen doors.

JOE: We have my job. We have each other. And there's one more thing. We have the right to live where we please. We're keeping all of those things, Anna.

ANNA: What have we done to hurt them?

JOE: Well, I guess maybe they think we've destroyed the dignity of their neighborhood, darling. That's why they've thrown garbage on our lawn.

ANNA: Dignity! Throwing garbage. Getting together a mob. Those are dignified things to do? Joe, how can you want to stay? How can you want to live on the same street with them? Don't you see what they are?

JOE: They're people, Anna. And I guess they're afraid, just as we are. That's why they've become a mob.

ANNA: What are they afraid of?

JOE: Living next door to someone they think is beneath them . . . an ex-convict . . . me.

ANNA: What do they think you did? They must think you're a thief or a murderer.

JOE: Maybe they do.

ANNA: Well, they can't. You'll tell them, Joe. It could have happened to any one of them. Tell them you're not a common criminal. You were in an accident, and that's all it was. They'll listen.

JOE: No, Anna.

ANNA: All you have to do is tell them, and they'll go away. It's not as if you committed a crime. You were speeding. Everybody speeds. You hit an old man, and he died. He walked right in front—

JOE: Anna, we have our freedom. If we beg for it, then it's gone. Don't you see that?

ANNA (*shouting*): No!

JOE: Listen, Anna, we're only little people, but we have certain rights. Judy's going to learn about them in school in a couple of years. They'll tell her that no one can take them away from her. She's got to be able to believe that. They include the right to be different. Well, a group of our neighbors have decided that we have to get out of here because they think we're different. They think we're not nice. Do we have to smile in their faces and tell them we are nice? We don't have to win the right to be free! It's the same as running away, Anna. It's staying on their terms. If we can't stay here on our terms, then there are no more places to stay anywhere. (*She begins to see it now, and she almost smiles.*) Now, we'll wait for them.

NARRATOR: From outside, we hear the tramping of feet in the distance. It grows louder.

JOE: Perhaps you should go into Judy's room.

ANNA: No, Joe. I want to watch you. I want to be proud.

NARRATOR: The tramping is now very loud. Suddenly it stops. For a moment there is silence. Then, from outside, we hear an angry voice.

CHARLIE DENTON: Joseph Blake! Come out here!

FIRST MAN: Come out of that house!

SECOND MAN: We want you, Joseph Blake.

FRANK: Come out—or we'll drag you out!

NARRATOR: The Blakes do not move. Suddenly a rock smashes through the window. The noise outside gets louder. Joe walks to the door.

ANNA: Joe!

NARRATOR: Joe flings the door open and steps outside. As he does so, the shouting stops. Joe stands in front of his house like a rock. He looks at the faces of his neighbors: the Morrisons—Frank, Clarice, and Roger—right in front of him. Charlie Denton is close behind. Mrs. Carson is there. And far to the rear are Arthur Hayes and Phyllis. One by one, people begin to speak again and shout.

FIRST MAN: Look at him, standing there as if he owns the block!

SECOND MAN: Who do you think you are—busting in where decent people live?

FIRST MAN: Go live with your own kind!

SECOND MAN: Your limousine is waiting, Mr. Blake. You're taking a one-way trip!

CHARLIE DENTON: What are we waiting for? Let's get him.

NARRATOR: The mob beings to move forward. Then, with a roar, Frank Morrison stops them.

FRANK: Quiet! Everybody shut up! *(The noise dies down.)* Now listen to me! This whole thing is going to be handled the way we planned. *(Roger looks up at Frank, seeing his father as a hero.)* This man is going to be asked politely to pack his things and get his family out of here. We don't have to tell him why. He knows that. He's going to be given a chance to leave right now. If he's got any brains in his head, he'll be out in one hour, and nobody will touch him. If he hasn't. . . . *(There is a threatening murmur from the crowd.)* Right! This thing is going to be done fair and square. *(He turns to Joe.)* What do you say, Mr. Blake?

NARRATOR: Joe stares at Frank. Arthur Hayes lowers his head and clenches his fists. He looks as if he wants to be sick. Finally, Joe speaks to Frank with a quiet fury that these people have never heard before.

JOE: I spit on your fairness! *(The crowd gasps.)* I own this house, and God gave me the right to live in it. Anyone who tries to take it away from me is going to have to climb over a pile of my bones to do it. You good people of Sycamore Street are going to have to kill me tonight! Are you ready, Mr. Morrison? Don't bother to be fair. You're the head man here. Be first!

NARRATOR: The crowd doesn't know what to do. Frank again calls for action, but not with the force he showed earlier.

FRANK: You heard him, everybody. Let's get him!

JOE: I asked for you first, Mr. Morrison!

FRANK *(to the crowd)*: Listen to me! Let's go, men!

NARRATOR: But the crowd is no longer moving as a whole.

CHARLIE DENTON: Don't let him throw you, Frank! He asked for it. Let's give it to him!

FRANK *(to crowd)*: Come on!

NARRATOR: He steps forward, but the people don't follow.

FRANK: What's the matter with you people?

JOE: They're waiting for you, Mr. Morrison.

NARRATOR: Frank turns and faces Joe, but does not move toward him. On the side, Charlie Denton picks up a stone.

CHARLIE *(throwing a stone)*: Let's start it, Frankie boy!

NARRATOR: The stone strikes Joe. Blood runs down the side of his face, but he stands firm. Arthur Hayes looks up in horror. Then a change comes over him. He moves forward. Phyllis tries to pull him back.

PHYLLIS *(screaming)*: Artie!

NARRATOR: But Artie breaks loose from her and pushes forward. Whoever is in his way is knocked aside. Finally he reaches Joe and stands next to him. He takes off his glasses and throws them into the crowd.

ARTHUR: Throw the next stone at me, neighbors! I live here, too!

NARRATOR: Now the crowd is unsure. Frank tries to rally them. As he begins to speak, Anna comes outside and stands proudly behind Joe and Arthur.

FRANK: Listen to me, you people! Let's remember what we came here to do! This man is garbage! He's ruining our neighborhood. Are we going to let him stop us? If we do, you know what will happen.

NARRATOR: Frank shouts on, running from person to person, as the crowd—ashamed—begins to drift away.

FRANK: You know what Sycamore Street will be like? I don't have to tell you. How do we know who will move in next? Listen, where are you going? We're all together in this! What about our kids? Our kids will be playing and going to school with his. How do you like that, neighbors? Come back here!

NARRATOR: But the crowd drifts away. Finally, only the Morrisons and Phyllis Hayes are left in the street. Joe, Anna, and Arthur watch them. Roger looks at his father. Then he turns away and takes Clarice's hand. His father is no longer the greatest guy in the world. Frank and his family walk slowly off. The Blakes turn and go into their house, leaving Arthur on the porch. Standing alone, in the middle of the street, is Phyllis.

ARTHUR (*sadly*): Well, what are you standing there for? My neighbor's head is bleeding!

NARRATOR: Then slowly, knowing that Arthur is no longer a grown-up child, Phyllis moves toward Joseph Blake's house.

THE END

CHECKING THE FACTS

1. Why doesn't Arthur Hayes want to take part in the "demonstration" against the Blakes? Why does Phyllis Hayes insist that they both take part?
2. Why are the Blakes unpopular on Sycamore Street?
3. Why does Anna Blake want to leave their house? Why does Joe Blake insist that they stay?
4. What happens when the mob arrives outside the Blake house?

INTERPRETING THE PLAY

1. Does Phyllis Hayes hate the Blakes, or is she afraid of them? Does she really know the Blakes? Does anyone on the block seem to know them very well?
2. What reason does Mrs. Carson give for visiting the Blakes? What are her real reasons? Do you think Joe Blake was right in ordering her to leave?
3. Joe Blake tells Frank Morrison, "I spit on your fairness!" What causes him to say this?
4. Why do you think Arthur takes a stand next to Joe Blake? Why do you think the mob stops listening to Frank Morrison—and drifts away?
5. Which characters, would you say, show courage in this teleplay?

WRITING

Suppose you live on Sycamore Street. You were *not* part of the mob that approached the Blakes, but you are shocked that some of your neighbors were. Write a letter to the editor of your local newspaper explaining why it is important to protect the "right" to be different.

THE PRIDE OF
JESSE HALLAM

a teleplay by Suzanne Clauser

CHARACTERS

JESSE HALLAM, a middle-aged man from Kentucky
TED, Jesse's 15-year-old son
JENNY, Jesse's 12-year-old daughter
MARION GALUCCI, the vice-principal at Ted's new school
SAL GALUCCI, Marion's father and the owner of a fruit and vegetable warehouse
MRS. KLEEMAN, a reading teacher
POLICEMAN

An old pickup truck stops in front of a hospital in Cincinnati, Ohio. The truck is loaded with the Hallam family's belongings. They have just moved here from Kentucky. Jesse Hallam and his two children get out. Jenny is wearing a large brace to hold her back straight. The Hallams go to the front desk in the hospital. A nurse gives Jesse a form to sign. Jesse doesn't know how to read, but he quickly signs the form and hands it back. Then he pulls out a thick roll of money.

JESSE: I always pay cash, ma'am. The doc said it would cost $14,000 for Jenny's operation, plus two months in the hospital. He also said we have to straighten out Jenny's backbone now. I'm ready to pay the whole cost in advance. *(He counts off $1,000 and puts it in his pocket.)* This will be enough for us to live on. *(He puts $14,000 on the desk.)* The rest is for Jenny's operation. I know you'll treat my baby right.

(Then Jesse and Ted go to Harding High School. Jesse speaks to the vice-principal, Marion Galucci.)

JESSE: I want to enroll my boy in your school. Here are his papers. *(He gives her an envelope.)*

MARION *(looking at the papers)*: This says he's in the tenth grade. We'll give him some tests to make sure what grade he should be in. Meanwhile, he can start in the tenth grade. There's no need for him to miss any school. *(She hands Jesse a printed form.)*

JESSE *(looking at it nervously)*: I'm sorry, but I don't have time for this. *(She frowns at him.)* I have to go job hunting.

MARION: This won't take long.

JESSE (*changing the subject*): I'll bet you know this town pretty well. Do you know where there's work?

MARION: Doing what?

JESSE: Anything—except coal mining. I've been doing that since I was 12. No more!

MARION: There are some factories out on Route 71. There's also the wholesale food market. It's only unskilled work, but you might go to Galucci's. That's my father's warehouse. He needs help.

JESSE: Thanks. I'd better get going. (*He hands the printed form to Ted.*) You can fill this out. (*He hurries off.*)
(*We see Jesse going to different factories. At each one, he is given a form to fill out. Each time, he throws away the form and leaves. He begins to feel depressed and angry.*)
(*A week later, Jesse and Ted are eating breakfast in their small apartment.*)

TED: I ran the mile in four and a half minutes yesterday. Can you believe it? You should have seen the coach's face. That track is as soft as a cloud compared to what we had in Kentucky. (*Pause.*) Are you going out to the factories again today?

JESSE: I've gone everywhere, and there aren't any jobs open. I'll try something closer in town. First, I'll stop by the hospital. (*Pause.*) Say, how were those tests you took at school? (*Ted frowns.*) Don't let that big school scare you. I'm sure you did great.
(*Jesse visits Jenny in the hospital.*)

JENNY (*frightened*): My operation is tomorrow.

JESSE: All the tests show that you're as healthy as a horse. So you're all ready for it.

JENNY: But I've been stuck in bed for a whole week. Afterward, I'll be stuck here for two more months.

JESSE: You've got to be patient. You've got to be stubborn, too, like your daddy. I'd have this operation for you, if I could. I'd do anything I could to make this better for you.

JENNY: There is one thing you could do. Mama used

to read to me, before she died. Could *you* read to me for a little while?

JESSE *(embarrassed):* I'm sorry, Jen, but I have a lot to do today. I'll be back tonight.

(Jesse is driving, looking lost. He goes through a red light, and a policeman stops him.)

JESSE: I'm sorry, officer, I saw the light too late.

POLICEMAN *(seeing Jesse's Kentucky license plates):* You out-of-town drivers don't know how to drive, that's all.

JESSE *(angry):* You've got no right to talk to me like that.

POLICEMAN: Just show me your license. *(Jesse hands over his license.)* This is seven months out of date!

JESSE *(embarrassed):* My wife used to keep track of it for me.

POLICEMAN: You're driving illegally in both Ohio and Kentucky. That will cost you $95. Mail it to this address. *(He hands Jesse a ticket.)* Don't let me catch you again without a proper license.

JESSE: How do I get an Ohio license?

POLICEMAN: Read the driver's handbook. The license bureau has them.

(Jesse goes home depressed. Ted gets home early from school.)

JESSE: I thought you had track practice.

TED *(upset):* I've been kicked out of school and off the team.

JESSE *(angry):* Didn't you have the sense not to cause trouble?

TED *(trying not to cry):* I didn't cause trouble! It was those tests! They say I can't read well enough! I have to go back to junior high!

JESSE *(feeling that he and Ted aren't being treated fairly):* I'm going to talk to that principal.

(Jesse tells the principal that it would be bad for Ted to change schools again. The track coach has already urged the principal to let Ted stay. The principal finally agrees.

85

But Ted can stay for only two months, until the end of the school year. And then he won't be promoted unless he does better on the standardized tests.)

(At 5:00 the next morning, Jesse goes to the wholesale food market, looking for work. He goes to the Galucci warehouse. Sal Galucci, an active man of 70, hires him to unload apples from a truck. Jesse looks closely at the apples.)

JESSE: Mr. Galucci, you want these apples to be top grade, don't you? Well, they've got worms in them. *(When Sal looks at the apples, he gets angry. He argues with the driver who brought the apples. Then he turns to Jesse.)*

SAL: I like the way you spot bad apples. Can you tell the difference between good and bad vegetables, too?

JESSE: I had a little farm in Kentucky. I raised all sorts of fruits and vegetables.

SAL: Why are you working on the loading dock? You're too old for that. And I'm too old to check the loads. I need someone to check them for me. Do you want the job?

JESSE: Yes, sir.

SAL: Let me show you around the warehouse.

JESSE: Fine, but I'll have to leave soon today. I have to go to the hospital. My little girl is having an operation today.

SAL *(smiling)*: Sure. You have to go care for your daughter. I have a daughter myself. Her name is Mariana. *(Jesse visits Jenny at the hospital. The operation turns out fine, but Jenny will have to stay in bed for two months.)*

(The next day, Jesse and Sal take a load of food to an outdoor market place. Sal tells Jesse to unload the food in the space market "Galucci." Jesse finds a space marked "Galiardi." When he starts to set up a booth there, Sal stops him.)

SAL: This says "Galiardi," not "Galucci." Can't you read? *(Jesse looks embarrassed.)* So you can't read. Why don't you learn? You aren't stupid. But it *is* stupid not to learn when you can. When I came to America, I couldn't read Italian, let alone English. I was 18 years old. I went to school with babies, but I learned!

JESSE: Sal, you can't teach an old dog new tricks.

SAL: That's only true if you believe it. You should go see my daughter Mariana. She'll find you lessons.

JESSE: I met Marion when Ted signed up for school. She and I don't really hit it off.

SAL: That's just Mariana's temper. She has a mind of her own. Since she was 12, she's called herself Marion, not Mariana. But she's got a good brain. If you want to work for Sal Galucci, you've got to read and write. I'll speak to her for you.

JESSE: I can speak for myself just fine.
(Jesse goes to Marion's office at Harding High School.)

MARION: Mr. Hallam, is there another problem with Ted?

JESSE: It's about me. You know I work for your daddy now. He said you can find me some lessons. I can't read or write.

MARION *(surprised)*: Why do you want to learn now, after so many years?

JESSE: I have to take a test for a driver's license.

MARION: Ted could help you with the handbook. He needs the reading practice anyway.

JESSE: I don't want Ted to know anything about this. Now, what about those lessons?

MARION: Learning to read takes time. It's hard work.

JESSE: Nobody ever said I was afraid of hard work. *(Pause.)* All my life I've been wanting to read.

MARION: How have you hidden this your whole life?

JESSE: You get cheated some, but you just keep trying to fake it.

MARION (*impressed by his pride and his courage*): All right. I'll find you reading lessons.

(*Next week, Jesse goes to a class of adults. The teacher goes very slowly through the alphabet. Some of the students look bored.*)

MRS. KLEEMAN: This letter is D. D is for "dog."

JESSE (*raising his hand*): Mrs. Kleeman, I know my ABC's already. I can even get the start of some words. I was hoping to learn some words straight away.

MRS. KLEEMAN: I know how hard it is for you to be patient. But we meet only twice a week. It will take a year or two before you can read or write well.

JESSE: I'm not sure I'll be in this town that long—unless it's in jail. (*He leaves the class.*)

(*A few days later, Marion and Sal are talking over breakfast.*)

SAL: Why don't you teach Jesse?

MARION: Papa, forget it. I haven't taught in years. Besides, it takes special skills to teach adults how to read.

SAL: You're smart. You could learn how to do it.

MARION: I already have a job.

SAL: Jesse is a good worker and a good man. I need him. He and I understand each other.

MARION: All right. I'll find him a private teacher.

SAL: Not just any teacher, Mariana—*you!*

(*A few days later, Jesse enters Marion's office.*)

JESSE: Your daddy says you found a teacher for me.

MARION: That's right. Sit down, and we'll get started.

JESSE (*surprised*): He didn't say it was going to be *you.*

MARION: I spent 15 hours this weekend learning how to teach you. So let's get started.

JESSE: Will this be faster than the class you sent me to?

MARION: I hope so. We'll meet more often. I also have a new method to try. You're an adult, not a child. You already know a lot of words in your head. I'll

89

show you how to match the words in your head with the words you see.

(A couple of hours pass. Jesse works very hard to learn the different sounds that letter combinations have. Marion is impressed by how hard he works and how much he learns. Finally, she hands him a sheet of paper.)

MARION: Read this word.

(Jesse struggles and figures it out.)

JESSE: "Promise."

MARION *(smiling)*: You've just read—*really* read your first word.

(Jesse smiles broadly.)
(Jesse and Marion work together for several weeks. Sometimes Jesse gets very frustrated and wants to quit. But he forces himself to go on.)
(Now Jesse enters her office for another lesson.)

MARION: Where were you yesterday?

JESSE: I went to Ted's track meet. I stopped by to tell you, but you weren't in.

MARION: You could have left me a note.

(Jesse suddenly realizes that he can write notes now.)

JESSE: I still have to get my driver's license. Can we work on that now?

MARION: That handbook is written at an eighth-grade level.

JESSE: I could make a list of the words I don't know. Then I could memorize the list.

MARION: There are some hard words in the handbook. Even I had to take the test twice to pass.

JESSE *(teasing)*: Even you?

(They smile at each other. They are good friends now.)
(Jesse visits Jenny in the hospital.)

JESSE: When you're better, the three of us can go to a Cincinnati Reds game.

JENNY: Can't we move back home?

JESSE *(surprised)*: We sold our house.

JENNY: Everything's different here. Even Ted seems different.

JESSE: He's making new friends at school. You will, too. *(He picks up a book from the bedside table.)* Are there any pictures in here?

JENNY: Sure. It's *The Wizard of Oz*.

(Jesse opens the book where her bookmark is.)

JESSE: Is this where you are?

JENNY: Yes. *(Pause.)* Are you going to read to me, Daddy?

JESSE: Why not? *(He looks at the page bravely, but nervously. Then he begins to read.)* "They saw running towards them two great beasts with bodies like bears and heads like tigers. 'They are the Kal-Kal-eye . . . . ' " *(He begins to panic.)* I know I've never seen that word before.

JENNY *(giggling)*: That's because they're magical beasts made up for this book. They're the Kalidahs.

JESSE *(relieved)*: I see *(He goes on reading.)* " 'They are the Kalidahs,' said the Cowardly Lion. 'Quick,' cried the Scarecrow, 'Lets us cross over the bridge.' "
(Jenny's eyes shine happily as her father reads to her.)
(Now Jesse is having another lesson with Marion.)

MARION: I want to give you something, Jesse. *(She looks for a certain book on her bookshelves.)*

JESSE *(looking at the bookshelves)*: Have you read all those books?

MARION: Most of them. You know, they contain a thousand different worlds—a thousand different lives. Now they can be yours, too. *(She hands him a book.)* Here's your first novel.

JESSE *(reading the title)*: "The Old Man and the Sea."

MARION: You can read this. The language is simple, and the man in the story is very much like you. He has a lot of pride.
(Jesse opens the book and begins to read it.)
(Later, Jesse goes to a track meet to watch Ted run, and Ted loses. Afterward Jesse tries to cheer him up.)

JESSE: You ran a good race.

TED: No, I didn't. I'm the one who lost the meet for us.

JESSE: You're not the only one on the team who lost points today. It's not all your fault.

TED: I guess not. But running is all I have going for me.

JESSE: I know it's hard to think you'll fail at the one thing you're doing right. But you've got more than running going for you.
(Ted doesn't look convinced.)

(A few days later, at work, Jesse is given an order to fill. He can't read the order form, so he takes it to Sal.)

JESSE *(frustrated)*: I can't read this, and I'm supposed to take that license test tomorrow!

SAL: It's just my bad handwriting you can't read. You can read out of a book. You're reading that book Marion gave you.

JESSE: I can't get through more than five pages an hour.

SAL: You have to think of what you *can* do, not what you *can't* do. If I hadn't thought about what I *could* do, I wouldn't be here with my own business.

(Jesse and Marion work together on the driver's handbook.)

JESSE *(reading)*: "Wait for a break in the traffic and move quietly—"

MARION *(correcting him)*: "Quickly."

JESSE *(sighs)*: I should know that word. It's one of the easy ones.

MARION: You're pushing yourself too hard. *(Pause.)* You know, you could enter the ninth grade next fall. *(Jesse looks surprised.)* All you need is a reading class this summer.

JESSE: That's crazy. How could I explain to Ted and Jenny that their daddy's starting ninth grade.

MARION: Stop that stupid shame! You're a proud man, and you've made a great deal of progress! You should be proud enough to tell the world about it! *(Jesse goes to take the driver's license test. He is so nervous that he panics, and he can't finish the test.)*

(Later, he tells Marion what happened.)

MARION: You can take it again.

JESSE: I don't know. The kids want to move back to Kentucky. Maybe that's what I should do.

MARION: You can't.

JESSE: There are two things I know I *can* do. I can go back home, and I can work in the coal mines.

94

MARION: You don't have to work in any coal mines. You've learned to read in less than two months. You're doing a great job for Papa. What would he do without you? He *cares* for you, Jesse.

JESSE: Marion, you taught me all I could learn. Because of you, I can hear voices in written words. I want to thank you for that.

MARION: I don't want your thanks. Just don't turn back. Everything is open for you.

(Jesse walks away.)

(Jenny and Ted are waiting for Jesse at the hospital. Ted has just gotten his report card, and he's afraid to show it to Jesse.)

JENNY: Did you really do *that* badly?

TED: It's the pits. I'm hoping Daddy won't get too mad since you're here. He's been in a bad mood ever since he decided to move back to Kentucky.

(Jesse walks in, smiling. He holds up an envelope.)

JESSE: I have three tickets to a Reds game in September. We can go when we drive back up here for Jenny's check-up. Well, Ted, how's your report card?

TED *(slowly)*: They flunked me. I told you, Daddy, running is all I had going for me. They put me back in ninth grade.

JESSE *(worried)*: What did you get—all F's?

TED: No. I got a D in math, and I got an A in gym.

JESSE: I don't understand it. I've seen you sitting over your books at night.

TED: It's all a bunch of junk. Anyway, what difference does it make? We're moving back home.

JESSE *(getting an idea)*: You got a D in arithmetic, but you got F's in biology, history, government, and English. Those are subjects you've got to read for, right?

(Ted nods, looking scared. Jesse picks up a Bible, opens it, and hands it to Ted.)

JESSE: Read me this Psalm.

TED *(nervously)*: Daddy, you know I can read.

JESSE: Let me hear you.

TED *(reading)*: "I waited pat—pat . . . . "

JESSE: "I waited patiently for the Lord." Go on.

TED *(reading)*: "And He in—increased . . . ."

JESSE: It's "inclined." Don't make up words that aren't there.

TED: You just have it memorized. *You* can't read at all.

JESSE *(shocked)*: How long have you known that?

TED: I always did. I saw that Mama did the accounts. You won't even write checks, because you can't write. You pay for everything in cash.

JENNY: But he *can* read. He reads to me all the time.

JESSE: I've only read to you lately, honey. I couldn't before then. The truth is, I've been taking lessons. *(He frowns at Ted.)* But in two months I've learned to read better than you. You say you'd be ashamed to go back to junior high, but you're facing a lifetime of worse shame. I'm surprised they'll let you into ninth grade at all.

(Two weeks later, Jesse and Ted are sitting in a classroom, waiting for their summer reading class to start. Ted looks embarrassed. Three 18-year-old boys are making a lot of noise. One of them plays a radio loudly. The teacher enters and tells the boy with the radio to turn it off. The boy just turns it up louder. Jesse has had enough. He walks over to the boy, grabs the radio, and turns it off. The students look amazed.)

JESSE: If you boys want to run away from words all your life, that's up to you. But you're not going to stop me or my son from learning how to read! *(He returns to his seat and Ted smiles proudly.)*

THE END

CHECKING THE FACTS

1. How does Jesse deal with the form he must sign at the hospital? What does he do with the form he's supposed to fill in at Ted's school?
2. Why does Jesse have a hard time finding a job? Why doesn't he realize that his driver's license has expired?
3. How does Sal Galucci figure out what Jesse's problem is?
4. Why is Ted doing poorly in school? How does Jesse figure out what Ted's problem is?
5. What do Jesse and Ted decide to do about the disadvantage they have in common?

INTERPRETING THE PLAY

1. Why do you think Sal Galucci cares so much about Jesse's ability to read?
2. Why do you think Marion goes to the trouble of teaching Jesse herself? What does she admire about him?
3. Why do you think it took Jesse so long to get help for his problem? Why did it take courage for him to admit he *had* this problem?

WRITING

Suppose you are Jesse. You have learned to read and write during summer school. Your final assignment is to write a short paper about the difference these skills will make in your life.

THE DIARY OF ANNE FRANK

a play by Frances Goodrich and Albert Hackett

CHARACTERS

MR. FRANK, a businessman
MRS. FRANK, his wife
ANNE FRANK, their 13-year-old daughter
MARGOT FRANK, their 18-year-old daughter
MR. VAN DAAN, another businessman
MRS. VAN DAAN, his wife
PETER VAN DAAN, their 16-year-old son
MR. DUSSEL, a dentist
MR. KRALER, Mr. Frank's business partner
MIEP GILES, a young woman who works with Mr. Kraler
ANNE'S VOICE, which reads parts of her diary

It is November, 1945, in Amsterdam, Holland. Mr. Frank enters an attic apartment. Some chairs are overturned. The curtains are tattered. Mr. Frank picks up a woman's glove from the floor, and tears fill his eyes. Miep Giles enters.

MIEP: Are you all right, Mr. Frank?

MR. FRANK: Yes, Miep. I've come here to say goodbye. I'm leaving Amsterdam. It has too many memories for me.

MIEP (*going to a shelf*): Some of your papers are here. We found them after you left.

MR. FRANK: Burn them.

MIEP: Should I burn this? (*She hands him a book.*)

MR. FRANK: It's Anne's diary. (*He opens it and reads.*) "Monday, July 6, 1942." That was only three years ago. Is it possible, Miep?
(*Anne's voice replaces his, as the lights go down.*)

ANNE'S VOICE: Dear Diary, I will start by telling you about myself. My name is Anne Frank, and I am 13 years old. Because my family is Jewish, we moved to Holland when Hitler came to power. My father

100

started a business, and all went well. Then, in 1940, the Dutch were defeated by the Germans. Things got very bad for the Jews. The Nazis forced Father out of business. We had to wear yellow Stars of David. Yesterday Father said we were going into hiding. We would hide in the attic of his office building. Three other people would join us—Mr. and Mrs. Van Daan and their son Peter.

(The lights come up. The attic is now clean and neat. It is three years earlier. The Van Daans are waiting for the Franks to arrive. They each wear a yellow star, showing that they are Jewish.)

MRS. VAN DAAN *(worried):* Mr. Frank said they'd be here at 7:00.

MR. VAN DAAN: They have two miles to walk.

MRS. VAN DAAN: Something has happened to them! They've been—

MR. VAN DAAN: I hear them coming upstairs.

(The Franks enter. Miep and Mr. Kraler are with them.)

MR. FRANK: Hello, Mr. and Mrs. Van Daan. I'm sorry we are late. There were many police on the streets. We had to take the long way around. This is my wife Edith. These are our daughters, Margot and Anne.

MR. VAN DAAN: I'm glad to meet you. This is my son Peter.

(They all shake hands with one another.)

MIEP: We put your food in this cupboard. I have to leave now. I must get ration books for you.

MRS. VAN DAAN: If the police see our ration books, won't they know we're here?

MIEP: The ration books won't have your names on them. Don't worry. *(She leaves.)*

MRS. FRANK: Will these be legal ration books? We've never done anything illegal before.

MR. FRANK: It isn't exactly legal for us to be living here in the first place.

MR. KRALER: I must leave, too. I should be downstairs in the office before the workers get here. Miep or I will be up here each day to bring you food and news. Good-bye for now. Oh, don't forget to tell them about the noise.

MR. FRANK: I'll tell them.

MRS. FRANK: Thank you so much for everything.

MR. KRALER: These are bad times when a man like

Mr. Frank must go into hiding. *(He leaves.)*

MR. FRANK: Let's take off some of these clothes.

(The Franks take off their coats. Underneath they are wearing several layers of clothing. They wore these clothes rather than carry suitcases, which would have attracted attention.)

MR. FRANK: Now, while the workers are in the building, we must be completely quiet. They arrive at 8:30 in the morning and leave at 5:30 at night. So from 8:00 until 6:00, we must move only when we have to. We can't wear shoes. We can't talk out loud. We can't turn on the water. This is how we must live until it is over.

MRS. FRANK: When will it be over?

(No one answers.)

MR. FRANK: After 6:00, we can move about. We can talk and laugh and have supper, just as we would at home. Now, it's almost 8:00. We should all get settled. Mr. and Mrs. Van Daan, your room is over there. The little one here is Peter's. The other one is Anne and Margot's. Edith and I will sleep out here.

MRS. VAN DAAN: Mr. Frank, you have saved our lives.

MR. FRANK: Your husband helped me when I first moved to this country. Now it is my turn to help you.

MRS. VAN DAAN *(to Peter)*: Will you be all right in that little room?

PETER *(embarrassed)*: Please, Mother, don't worry.

(Mr. and Mrs. Van Daan go into their room.)

MR. FRANK: Anne and Peter, take off your shoes now.

(He takes Mrs. Frank and Margot into Margot and Anne's room.)

(Anne and Peter take off their shoes. Then Peter opens a carrying case and takes out a cat.)

ANNE *(delighted)*: What's your cat's name?

103

PETER *(shy)*: Mouschi.

ANNE: I love cats. I had to leave my cat behind. I'm going to miss her terribly. *(She picks up Mouschi, but Peter takes him from her.)*

PETER: Mouschi doesn't like strangers.

ANNE: Then I'll have to stop being a stranger, won't I? Where did you go to school?

PETER: The Jewish high school.

ANNE: That's where Margot and I went, but I never saw you.

PETER: I used to see you. You were always with a crowd of kids.

ANNE: Why didn't you join us?

PETER: I'm a loner. *(He starts to rip off the yellow star from his sweater.)*

ANNE: You can't do that. They'll arrest you if you go out without your star.

PETER: Who's going out?

ANNE: You're right. We don't need them anymore. *(She rips the star off her blouse.)* What are you going to do with yours?

PETER: Burn it!

ANNE: I can't throw mine away.

PETER: Why not? They made you wear it so they could spit on you!

ANNE: I know, but it *is* the Star of David.
(Mr. Frank enters.)

MR. FRANK: Peter, we must find a bed for your cat. *(He finds a small washtub and gives it to Peter.)* Will he be comfortable in that?

PETER: Yes. Thanks. *(He takes the cat and the washtub into his room.)*

MR. FRANK: Peter is a nice boy.

ANNE: He's awfully shy.

MR. FRANK: You'll like him.

ANNE: I hope so. He's the only boy I'll see for a long time.

105

MR. FRANK: Anne, there's a box over there. Will you open it?

(Anne opens the box and takes out a diary.)

ANNE: It's a diary! I've always wanted one. *(She heads for the door to the stairs.)* I'm going down to the office for a pencil.

MR. FRANK *(grabbing her arm)*: Anne! No!

ANNE: But there's no one in the building now.

MR. FRANK: I don't want you ever to go beyond that door. It isn't safe. It will be hard, I know. But we can be free in certain ways. No locks will be put on our minds. Miep will bring us books, and we can read. It won't be so bad here. After all, you won't have to practice the piano.

(Anne smiles at her father. Then the lights go down.)

ANNE'S VOICE: Friday, August 21, 1942. I'll describe how it feels to be in hiding. It's the silence of the night that frightens me most. Every time I hear a creak in the building, I'm sure they're coming for us. The days aren't as bad. At least Miep and Mr. Kraler are downstairs, protecting us. I asked Father what would happen to them if the Nazis found out they are hiding us. He said they would be treated as badly as we would be.

(The lights come up. Everyone in the attic is waiting for the last worker to leave at 6:00 p.m. Mr. Frank, holding his shoes, watches out the window.)

MR. FRANK: It's safe now.

(Everyone relaxes. Anne hides Peter's shoes behind her back.)

PETER: Anne, have you seen my shoes?

ANNE: Your shoes?

PETER: You've taken them, haven't you?

ANNE: I don't know what you're talking about.

(Peter grabs her and tries to get his shoes from her.)

MRS. FRANK: Anne and Peter, stop it!

(Peter looks embarrassed. Anne gives him his shoes.)

106

ANNE: Peter, will you dance with me?

PETER *(angry)*: I've told you that I don't know how to dance. I'm going to give Mouschi his supper. *(He disappears into his room.)*

MRS. FRANK: I wish you'd act more grown up, Anne.

ANNE: I only wanted some fun after sitting still all day. *(As Margot walks by, Anne catches hold of her.)* Margot, please dance with me.

MARGOT *(pulling away)*: I have to help fix supper.

(Anne sings to herself and dances across the room. Mr. Frank holds out his arms, and they dance together. When they finish, they take a bow. Mrs. Van Daan comes out of her room.)

MRS. VAN DAAN: I'll bet Peter hasn't finished his homework. Anne, will you get him out here, please?

ANNE *(dancing to Peter's door)*: Your mother says to get out here.

PETER *(opening the door a bit)*: I have to feed Mouschi.

ANNE: I'll feed Mouschi.

PETER: I don't want you in here!

MRS. VAN DAAN: Peter!

PETER: All right. *(He comes out of the room.)*

MRS. VAN DAAN: Peter, that's no way to treat your little girlfriend.

PETER *(embarrassed)*: Mother, will you stop saying that?

MRS. VAN DAAN: He acts as if it's something to be ashamed of. You shouldn't be ashamed to have a little girlfriend.

PETER: You're crazy. She's only 13.

ANNE: Of all the boys in the world, why do I get locked up with you?

(Mrs. Frank goes to Anne and starts to fix her hair.)

MRS. FRANK: Anne, your forehead is warm. You don't have a fever, do you?

ANNE *(impatient)*: No, Mother.

MRS. FRANK: We can't call a doctor here, you know. So we must prevent an illness before it comes. Let me see your tongue.

ANNE: Mother, don't treat me like a baby. *(But she sticks out her tongue.)*

MRS. FRANK: You seem all right.

MR. FRANK: There's nothing the matter with Anne that a ride on her bike or a visit with her friends wouldn't cure. Isn't that so?

(Anne nods. Mr. Van Daan comes out of his room.)

109

MR. VAN DAAN: What's for supper tonight?

MRS. VAN DAAN: Beans.

MR. VAN DAAN: Not again!

MRS. VAN DAAN: What can we do? That's all that Miep brought.

MR. FRANK (*looking up from some papers*): Anne, you got an A on your history paper today. You got a B in Latin.

MARGOT: How did I do?

ANNE (*patting Margot on the head*): Excellent! Excellent! Excellent!

(*Margot brushes her hand away.*)

MR. FRANK: You made some mistakes in your Latin. Let me show you. (*He and Margot go off to discuss the lesson.*)

ANNE: Mrs. Van Daan, may I try on your fur coat?

MRS. FRANK: No, Anne.

MRS. VAN DAAN: It's all right, but be careful. My father gave me that coat. He always bought me the best that money could buy.

ANNE: Did you have a lot of boyfriends before you were married?

MRS. FRANK: Don't ask personal questions, Anne. It's not polite.

MRS. VAN DAAN (*helping Anne put on the fur coat*): I don't mind. Yes, Anne, our house was always filled with boys when I was young.

MR. VAN DAAN: Oh, no, here we go again.

MRS. VAN DAAN: When I was 16, I had good legs. I still do. I may not be as pretty as I used to be, but I still have good legs. Don't you think so, Mr. Frank?

PETER: Mother, please!

MRS. VAN DAAN: Oh, so I embarrass you, do I?

MR. VAN DAAN: Stop talking that way in front of Anne. Don't you know she writes everything down in her diary?

110

MRS. VAN DAAN: What if she does? I'm only telling the truth.

MR. VAN DAAN *(to Anne):* Why are you staring at us?

ANNE: I've never heard grown-ups quarrel before. I thought only children quarreled.

MRS. FRANK *(changing the subject):* Anne, will you bring me my knitting?

ANNE *(taking her mother's knitting to her):* Mother, did you know that Miep is engaged? Her boyfriend's name is Dirk. She's afraid the Nazis will send him away to work in a gun factory. *(She starts to drink a glass of milk.)*

MR. VAN DAAN: Anne, don't you ever get tired of talking? Why aren't you nice and quiet like your sister Margot? Men don't like girls who show off.

ANNE: I don't want to be a quiet girl. I want to be a famous dancer or singer. *(She starts to dance around the room—and spills her glass of milk on Mrs. Van Daan's fur coat.)* Oh, I am so sorry!

MRS. VAN DAAN: You clumsy fool! Do you know what that coat cost? I could kill you! *(She runs into her room, and her husband follows her to calm her down.)*

ANNE: I didn't mean to. It was an accident. Anyone can have an accident.

MRS. FRANK: But you must not argue with them. They are our guests. Besides, we are all living under great strain. We must control ourselves. You don't hear Margot getting into fights with them, do you?

ANNE: That's all I hear—how wonderful Margot is. Everything she does is right. Everything I do is wrong. *(She runs into her room.)*

MRS. FRANK: I don't know how we can go on living this way. I can't say a word to Anne. She gets so angry with me.

MARGOT: You know Anne. In half an hour, she'll be out here laughing and joking again.

(The door buzzer goes off. Everyone hurries into the center room. Mr. Kraler enters.)

MR. VAN DAAN: How are you, Mr. Kraler?

MR. KRALER: I have something to talk over with you. Today Dirk, Miep's boyfriend, stopped by. He has a Jewish friend who needs a hiding place. I know it's a lot to ask of you, but could you take him in?

MR. FRANK: Of course we will.

MR. KRALER: It will only be for a night or two, until I find another place. I'll bring him up. He's downstairs. His name is Jan Dussel, and he's a dentist. *(He goes downstairs.)*

MR. FRANK: I spoke without asking the rest of you. But I knew you'd feel as I do.

MR. VAN DAAN: This is your place. You have a right to do as you please. But we have so little food.

MR. FRANK: We can stretch the food. It's only for a few days.

MR. VAN DAAN: Do you want to make a bet? If Mr. Kraler can't find another hiding place, Dussel might stay here forever.

MRS. FRANK: I think it's fine to have him. But where will he sleep? Peter's room is too small for a man. I guess Margot could move in here with us. Then Mr. Dussel could have her bed.

MR. FRANK: Anne, you don't mind sharing your room with Mr. Dussel, do you?

ANNE *(pretending not to mind):* No. Of course not.
(Mr. Kraler brings Mr. Dussel upstairs and introduces him to everyone.)

MR. DUSSEL *(to Mr. Kraler):* What can I say to thank you?

MRS. FRANK: We couldn't live without Mr. Kraler and Miep.

MR. KRALER: You make us seem heroic, but it isn't that at all. We simply don't like the Nazis. I must go. Good night. *(He leaves.)*

113

MR. DUSSEL: Mr. Frank, I heard you had escaped to Switzerland. A woman told me she had gone to your house. She found a piece of paper with a Swiss address on it. She thought that's where you had gone.

ANNE: Father left that address there so people would believe that. It worked, Father!

MR. VAN DAAN: Mr. Dussel, did Mr. Kraler warn you that you don't get much to eat here?

MR. DUSSEL: You don't realize what is going on outside. If you did, you wouldn't worry about not having enough food. Right here in Amsterdam hundreds of Jews disappear every day. They get a call-up notice. If you ignore the notice, the Nazis drag you from your home. They send you to a death camp!

MRS. FRANK: We didn't know that things had gotten so much worse.

MR. FRANK: I'm sure that Mr. Dussel would like to get settled before supper. We can ask him questions later. Anne, will you show Mr. Dussel to his room? *(Anne shows Mr. Dussel their room.)*

ANNE: Here we are. You're going to share the room with me.

MR. DUSSEL: I have always lived alone. I haven't learned to adjust to other people. I hope you'll put up with me until I learn.

ANNE: I hope I won't bother you.

MR. DUSSEL: I get along very well with children. *(The lights go down.)*

ANNE'S VOICE: Mr. Dussel and I had another battle yesterday. He doesn't like my appearance, my character, or my manners. Sometimes I think I'm going to hit him. *(The lights come up. Anne is in bed, having a nightmare.)*

ANNE (*screaming*): No! Don't take me!

MR. DUSSEL (*getting out of bed*): Anne! Be quiet! Someone outside the building will hear you!

(*Mrs. Frank runs in and shakes Anne awake.*)

MRS. FRANK: It's all right, Anne.

MR. DUSSEL: Something must be done about that child yelling like that. Somebody outside might hear her. She's putting our lives in danger.

MRS. FRANK (*to Anne*): Was it a bad dream?

ANNE: I'd rather not talk about it.

MRS. FRANK: I'll sit here until you go back to sleep.

ANNE: I'd rather you didn't. Would you ask Father to come here?

MRS. FRANK: All right. (*She goes to the center room, where Mr. Frank and Margot are.*) Go to her, Otto. She is still shaking with fear.

(*Mr. Frank goes into Anne's room.*)

MRS. FRANK (*to Margot*): She wants nothing to do with me.

MARGOT: It's a phase. She'll get over it.

(*Meanwhile, Mr. Frank comforts Anne.*)

ANNE: I dreamed that the police came to get us. They broke down the door and grabbed me. They started to drag me out.

MR. FRANK: Lie quietly now. Try to sleep.

ANNE: I'm a terrible coward. I think I'm grown up. Then something happens, and I run to you like a baby. I love you, Father.

MR. FRANK: It's fine to hear you say that. But I'll be much happier if you say you love your mother, too.

ANNE: She doesn't understand me.

MR. FRANK: You hurt her very much right now.

ANNE: I was horrible, wasn't I? The worst thing is that I can see myself being mean. (*Pause.*) I have a nice side, but I'm afraid to show it. I'm afraid people will laugh at me if I'm serious. So "the mean Anne"

shows up on the outside, and "the good Anne" stays on the inside. I keep trying to change them around.

(The lights go down.)

ANNE'S VOICE: November 9, 1942. The air raids are getting worse. But Father says that means the war will end soon. Just for fun, he asked each of us what we wanted to do when we get out of here. Mrs. Van Daan wants to be home with her own things . . . "the best that money could buy." Peter would like to go to the movies. I'd like to ride my bike and laugh until my belly aches and be with my friends.

(The lights come up. It is now December, and the families are having a Hanukkah dinner. Anne surprises everyone with gifts she has made. She hands a book to Margot.)

MARGOT: It's a new crossword puzzle book. Where did you get it?

ANNE: It's not new. I erased all the answers. Now you can do them all over again. *(She hands her mother a note.)*

MRS. FRANK *(reading it):* "Here is an I.O.U. that I promise to pay, ten hours of doing whatever you say. Signed, Anne Frank."

MR. DUSSEL: You wouldn't like to sell that, would you, Mrs. Frank?

MRS. FRANK: This is the most precious gift I've ever had.

ANNE *(handing her father a scarf):* I made it out of odds and ends. I knitted each night in the dark. I'm afraid it looks better in the dark. *(She hands Peter a gift for Mouschi.)*

MR. VAN DAAN: That cat eats too much. We're getting rid of it tonight!

PETER: No. If he goes, I go.

MRS. VAN DAAN: You're not going, and the cat's not going.

117

(Suddenly they hear a crash from below. Peter reaches up to turn off the lamp. He accidentally hits the metal lamp shade, which crashes to the floor. They hear someone running down the stairs in the building below. The footsteps die away.)

MR. FRANK: I think they're gone.

MRS. VAN DAAN: I'll bet it was the police. They heard us, and they've gone to get help.

MR. FRANK: It could have been a thief. I'll go down and check. *(He goes downstairs.)*

MRS. VAN DAAN *(terrified):* Let's get our money. I've heard you can bribe the police to let you go.

MR. VAN DAAN: Keep still!

MRS. VAN DAAN: Do you want to be dragged off to a concentration camp? Are you going to stand there and wait for them to come and get you?

MR. VAN DAAN: Be quiet!

(Mrs. Frank begins to pray. She stops when Mr. Frank comes back.)

MR. FRANK: It was a thief. He took the cash box and the radio.

MR. DUSSEL: And now someone knows we're up here.

MRS. VAN DAAN: Do you think a thief would go to the police? Would he say, "I was robbing a place, and I heard noise upstairs"?

MR. DUSSEL: Someday he may be caught. Then he might make a deal with the police. If they let him off, he'll tell them where some Jews are hiding.

ANNE: Father, we can't stay here now.

MR. VAN DAAN: There's no place we can go.

MR. FRANK: We must not lose our courage. Let us give thanks to God that we are still alive.

(As they all pray together, the lights go down.)

ANNE'S VOICE: January 1, 1944. We have been here for one year, five months, and 25 days. The Van Daans still have their arguments. Mother and I still

don't understand each other. But I feel I have been changing—growing up.

(The lights come up, and the door buzzer goes off. Miep and Mr. Kraler arrive with some food.)

MR. KRALER: We came to bring all of you New Year's greetings.

ANNE: It's wonderful to see you. I can smell the wind and cold on your clothes.

PETER: Miep, have you been able to find Mouschi?

MIEP: I'm sorry, Peter. I asked around the neighborhood, but nobody has seen a gray cat.

MR. FRANK: Look what Miep has brought us—a cake!

119

MRS. FRANK: It's beautiful.

MRS. VAN DAAN: It's been ages since I've had cake. *(She gets out a knife as others set the table.)*

MR. DUSSEL: Mrs. Frank should cut the cake.

MRS. VAN DAAN: What's the difference?

MR. DUSSEL: Mrs. Frank divides things better.

MRS. VAN DAAN: Don't I always give everyone the same share?

MR. DUSSEL: Mr. Van Daan always gets a little bit more.

MR. VAN DAAN: That's a lie!

MR. FRANK: Please! Do you see what a little cake does to us? It goes right to our heads. *(They calm down and eat the cake in peace.)*

PETER: Miep, maybe Mouschi went back to our house. Would you have time to look there?

MIEP: I'll try.

MR. DUSSEL: Face it. Someone has made a meal of that cat! *(Peter looks as if he'd like to hit Mr. Dussel.)*

MIEP: I have to go. Good-bye. *(She leaves.)*

MR. KRALER: Mr. Frank, may I speak to you alone?

MARGOT: What is it? Something has gone wrong, hasn't it?

MR. KRALER: A week ago, a man who works in the storeroom asked me, "How is Mr. Frank?" He had heard you had gone to Switzerland. He said he thought I might know more about it. Then he started staring at the bookcase—the one that hides the door to this attic. He asked me what happened to the door that used to be there. Then he asked me for a big raise.

MR. VAN DAAN: That's blackmail!

MR. DUSSEL: He might have been the thief we heard. Pay him what he asks. We have no choice.

MR. FRANK: Offer him half of what he asks.

MR. KRALER: I'll try that. I'm not sure how much he

knows. If he knows anything, he'll ask for more later. Good-bye. *(He leaves.)*

MARGOT: Sometimes I wish the end would come—whatever it is. Then at least we'd know where we were.

MRS. FRANK: Think how lucky we are! Thousands die in the war every day. Others die in concentration camps.

ANNE *(angrily)*: What's the good of thinking sad thoughts when you're already sad? You grown-ups have had your chance. But Margot and Peter and I are young. We're trying to hold onto our ideals, when everything else is being destroyed. It isn't our fault the world is in such a mess! *(She runs into her room, and Peter follows.)*

PETER: You were fine just now. You know how to talk to them.

ANNE: I go too far. I hurt people's feelings.

PETER: If it weren't for you, I couldn't stand it here.

ANNE *(surprised)*: Thank you. I get so angry. They've already formed their opinions. We're still trying to find things out. We have problems here that no people our age have ever had.

PETER: At least you can talk to your father.

ANNE: Yes, but nothing can take the place of friends. It's funny—this is the first time you and I have really talked. It helps to have someone to talk to.

PETER: You can talk to me anytime.

(The lights go down.)

ANNE'S VOICE: We have gotten bad news. The people who got ration books for us have been arrested. We have had to cut down on food. Our stomachs are so empty that they make strange noises. I feel that spring is almost here. I need to talk to someone—someone young.

(The lights come up. Anne walks across the center room. Mrs. Van Daan watches her enter Peter's room.)

121

MRS. VAN DAAN: In my day, the boys called on the girls.

MRS. FRANK: Peter's room is the only place where they can talk. Anne won't stay long. She must go to bed at 9:00.

(In Peter's room, Anne and Peter talk.)

ANNE: Aren't they awful? They treat us like children.

PETER: Don't let it bother you.

ANNE: They remember what they were like at our age, but we are different. Sometimes I'd like to go back to my old life for a few days. But after that, I'd be bored. I think about life more seriously now. I want to be a writer. What do you want to do?

PETER: I might work on a farm. I know I'm not smart.

ANNE: That isn't true. You're better than I am at algebra. So is Margot. Margot is so good. She's sweet and bright and beautiful, and I'm not.

PETER: I don't agree. I think you're pretty.

ANNE: That's not true.

PETER: You've changed since we moved in here. I used to think you were too noisy. Now you're quieter.

ANNE: I'll bet you'll never think of me after we leave here. You'll go back to your friends and wonder what you saw in me.

PETER: I haven't got any friends. I can get along without them.

ANNE: Can you get along without me? I'm your friend.

PETER: If they were all like you, it would be different.

ANNE: It's 9:00, so I have to go. Maybe I'll bring my diary next time. There's a lot in it about you. I used to think you were a nothing, the way you thought I was.

PETER: Did you change your mind?

ANNE *(smiling):* You'll see.

(Peter suddenly kisses her briefly. She leaves his room in a daze.)

MRS. VAN DAAN *(watching Anne):* Ah, ha!

122

(The lights go down.)

ANNE'S VOICE: Thursday, April 20, 1944. Rats have taken some of our food again. Even Mr. Dussel now wishes that Mouschi were here. The Allies are getting closer. Miep says that people talk of nothing else. Life has become better for me. I often go to Peter's room after supper. Life is easier when you have someone you can talk to.

(Moonlight comes through the skylight. Otherwise, the attic rooms are dark. Mr. Van Daan tiptoes across the center room. He opens the cupboard and takes out some bread. Mrs. Frank sits up in bed and sees him.)

MRS. FRANK: Otto! Mr. Van Daan is stealing the food!

(The others run into the room. Margot turns on a lamp.)

MR. DUSSEL: So it was you, Mr. Van Daan! We thought it was rats making our bread disappear.

MR. FRANK: How could you do such a thing?

MR. VAN DAAN: I'm hungry.

MRS. FRANK: We are all hungry. The children get thinner every day. You have been stealing food from the children!

MRS. VAN DAAN: He needs more food. He's a big man.

MRS. FRANK: I've seen you, Mrs. Van Daan. You save extra food for your husband. I've stayed quiet, but not any longer. I want him to get out of here.

MR. FRANK: Edith, you are speaking in anger. For two years we have lived here in peace. Mr. Van Daan, this won't happen again, will it?

MR. VAN DAAN: No. No. *(He looks very ashamed as he goes to his room.)*

MRS. FRANK: I want them to leave. There are other hiding places.

MRS. VAN DAAN: Mr. Frank, do you remember how my husband helped you when you first came to Amsterdam?

MRS. FRANK: My husband had paid off that debt to

123

you many times over. I should have spoken out long ago.

MR. DUSSEL: You can't be nice to some people.

MRS. VAN DAAN *(to Mr. Dussel):* There would have been plenty to eat if you hadn't moved in!

MR. FRANK: We don't need the Nazis to destroy us. We are destroying ourselves.

MRS. FRANK *(handing money to Mrs. Van Daan):* Give this to Miep. She'll find a hiding place for you.

ANNE: Mother, you can't put Peter out. He hasn't done anything.

MRS. FRANK: He can stay, of course.

PETER: If Father goes, I wouldn't feel right staying here.

ANNE *(to her mother):* I don't care about the food! They can have mine! Just don't send them away!

MRS. FRANK: They'll stay here until Miep finds them a hiding place. But Mr. Van Daan must never go near our food supply again.

(The door buzzer sounds, and everyone freezes. Then Mr. Frank goes to the door, and Miep enters.)

MIEP: I have wonderful news! The invasion has begun. The Allies have landed in France. The war will soon be over!

(Everyone cheers. The adults hug one another, their anger and fears forgotten. The lights go down.)

ANNE'S VOICE: Friday, August 4, 1944. Miep says the police found the radio that was stolen. Mr. Dussel says they'll trace it back to the thief, and the thief will tell them where we are. Everyone is feeling low. I have often felt low, but I have never felt despair. I can shake off everything if I write. But will I ever be able to write well? I hope so. I want to go on living after my death.

(The lights come up. Everyone is in the center room. There is a feeling of tension.)

MR. DUSSEL: Something must have happened, Mr.

Frank. Miep hasn't been to see us in three days. Today no workers have come to the office.

MR. FRANK: Maybe it's Sunday. Maybe we've lost track of the days.

MR. DUSSEL: I don't lose track. It's Friday. Something must have happened.

MR. VAN DAAN: I suppose we just have to wait here until we die.

MRS. VAN DAAN: I can't stand it!

MR. VAN DAAN: It's your fault we're here. We could have been safe in Switzerland or America. But you wouldn't leave when I wanted to. You couldn't leave your precious belongings.

(Peter is embarrassed by their fighting. He goes into his room. Anne follows him and tries to cheer him up.)

ANNE *(looking up at the skylight)*: Look at the sky, Peter. Aren't the clouds beautiful? I used to take nature for granted. Now I'm crazy about it.

PETER: I think I'm going crazy—really! I can't stand much more of this.

ANNE: I wish you had something to believe in. Think of the poeple who risk their lives for us every day. When I think of that, I'm not afraid anymore.

PETER: Well, when I begin to think, I get angry. We've been hiding here for two years. We're trapped here, just waiting for them to get us.

ANNE: We're not the only people who have had to suffer.

PETER: That doesn't make me feel any better.

ANNE: Do you know what I think? I think the world is going through a phase, the way I did with Mother. It will pass someday. In spite of everything, I still believe that people are really good at heart.

PETER: I want to see something good *now,* not a thousand years from now.

ANNE: Listen to us. We're arguing like a couple of stupid grown-ups. Someday, when we're—

(Suddenly they hear several cars pull up outside the building. A doorbell rings downstairs. Then they hear a door being battered down. Everyone gathers in the center room. Footsteps are heard running up the stairs. The lights go down.)

ANNE'S VOICE: Our stay here is over. They have given us five minutes to get our things. We can each take a bag of clothing, nothing else. So, Dear Diary, I must leave you behind. Miep, if you should find this diary, keep it for me. I hope someday—
(The lights come up. Now we see the attic as it was in the first scene. Mr. Kraler has joined Miep and Mr. Frank.)

MR. FRANK *(closing Anne's diary):* There is no more.

MIEP: I had gone to the country to find food that day. When I got back here, the block was surrounded by police.

MR. KRALER: The thief had told them where you were.

MR. FRANK: First they took us to a camp in Holland. Anne was actually happy there. After two years of being shut up, she loved being outside in the sunshine. Then we were sent to Poland. The men went to Auschwitz, and the women went to Belsen. I was set free in January. Whenever I met people, I'd ask for news of my family. That's how I learned about my wife's death. I heard that Margot, Peter, the Van Daans, and Mr. Dussel had died, too. But I heard nothing about Anne. I still had hope. Yesterday I went to Rotterdam. I had heard of a woman there who was in Belsen with Anne. She told me that Anne was dead. *(He looks at the diary.)*

ANNE'S VOICE: In spite of everything, I still believe that people are really good at heart.

MR. FRANK: She puts me to shame.

THE END

CHECKING THE FACTS

1. When does Mr. Frank find Anne's diary? When did the Franks go into hiding?
2. Why do the Van Daans share the hiding place with the Franks? Why does Mr. Dussel join them?
3. Who is downstairs during the Hanukkah dinner? How and why does that person try to blackmail Mr. Kraler?
4. Mr. and Mrs. Frank seem amazingly calm and generous while living under great tension. What finally makes Mrs. Frank so angry that she tells Mr. Van Daan that he must leave the hiding place?
5. What finally happens to each person who hid in the attic rooms?

INTERPRETING THE PLAY

1. Why would it be so difficult to live in the attic rooms? What things couldn't you do? What dangers would haunt you? Why would it be hard to live so closely with "strangers"?
2. Why does Anne often feel "different" or "apart" from the others? Why do you think she and Peter are drawn toward each other?
3. After Mrs. Frank tells Mr. Van Daan that he must leave, Mr. Frank says, "We don't need the Nazis to destroy us. We are destroying ourselves." What does he mean?

WRITING

Suppose you had been in hiding for two years. What is the first thing you would do when you got your freedom? Write about it briefly.